THE LAW AND THE CHRISTIAN

GOD'S LIGHT WITHIN GOD'S LIMITS

KEN CASILLAS

UNIVERSITY PRESS

Greenville, South Carolina

Library of Congress Cataloging-in-Publication Data

Casillas, Ken, 1970-
  The law and the Christian : God's light within God's limits / Ken Casillas.
      p. cm.
  Summary: "This book studies the relationship of the Mosaic law to the New
Testament Christian"—Provided by publisher.
  ISBN 978-1-59166-797-1 (perfect bound pbk. : alk. paper)
  1. Law and gospel. 2. Bible. O.T.—Relation to the New Testament. I. Title.
  BT79.C37 2007
  241'.2—dc22

                                                                    2007022025

All Scripture is quoted from the Authorized King James Version unless otherwise noted.

NASB: Scripture taken from the NEW AMERICAN STANDARD BIBLE®, Copyright © 1960, 1962, 1963, 1968, 1971, 1972, 1973, 1975, 1977, 1995 by The Lockman Foundation. Used by permission.

The fact that materials produced by other publishers may be referred to in this volume does not constitute an endorsement of the content or theological position of materials produced by such publishers.

The Law and the Christian:
God's Light Within God's Limits

Ken Casillas, PhD

Design by Peter Crane
Page layout by Kelley Moore

© 2007 BJU Press
Greenville, South Carolina 29614
Bob Jones University Press is a division of BJU Press

ISBN 978-1-59166-797-1

15   14   13   12   11   10   9   8   7   6   5   4   3   2   1

To Dr. Robert D. Bell,
my professor and mentor,
who has labored tirelessly
to train a generation
of preachers and teachers
to mine the riches
of Old Testament revelation

CONTENTS

PREFACE

Faithful Christians in every generation hunger for *Biblical Discernment for Difficult Issues*, the title of this book series authored by the faculty of Bob Jones University Seminary. The true disciple thirsts for a life that reflects Christ's love for others while striving to maintain loyalty to God's revealed Truth, the Scriptures. But as every mature Christian soon learns, demonstrating both God's compassion and God's holiness in this life is a balance that is never easy to strike.

Our propensity to wander from the right path is enough to alarm any honest follower of Christ. How quickly in our pursuit of holiness we do race into the darkness of a harsh, unforgiving condemnation of others who somehow lack the light we enjoy. And how tragically inclined we all are to slip, while on the narrow way, from the firm ground of genuine compassion into the mire of an unbiblical naiveté or an unwise sentimentality. Only by God's grace can the believer combine that loving compassion and that pursuit of a rigorous holiness into one life to bring the true "light of the knowledge of the glory of God in the face of Jesus Christ" to a needy church and a lost world.

The aim of this series is to provide help in finding this right, discerning balance in spiritual life without sacrificing one crucial emphasis in Scripture for another. While written in an easy-to-read style, these works attempt to combine mature, penetrating theological thought with thorough research. They aim to provide both a fact-intensive exposition of Scripture and a piercing application of it to real human experience. Hopefully those who read will find themselves making significant strides forward on the way to a renewed mind and a transformed life for the glory of Christ.

Stephen J. Hankins, Dean
Bob Jones University Seminary

1

INTRODUCTION

It's funny what you remember from your childhood. Personally, I find it difficult to recall specific conversations, events, and experiences. But of all the positive things I would like to remember from my years as a missionary child in Puerto Rico, for some reason the sad story of Karl Wallenda has stayed with me. Wallenda was a German entertainer who became famous for doing extremely dangerous tightrope stunts without a safety net. His family act was dubbed the Flying Wallendas, and their signature performance was a seven-person pyramid topped by a woman standing on a chair. The Wallendas performed internationally through the middle of the twentieth century. Though the group survived catastrophes such as the 1944 Hartford circus fire, in 1962 Karl lost his son-in-law and nephew in a major fall in Detroit. Overcoming a cracked pelvis, Karl continued his death-defying stunts. At sixty-five he traversed a distance of 1200 feet above Georgia's Tallulah Falls Gorge, doing two headstands some 700 feet in the air.

Wallenda walked for the last time at the age of seventy-three. For a promotional event, a wire was strung about 120 feet high between two hotels in San Juan, Puerto Rico. Some believe the problem was the high ocean winds. The family says that some guy ropes were misconnected. Whatever the case, Karl Wallenda plunged to his death on March 22, 1978. The entertainer once said, "Life is being on the wire; everything else is just waiting."[1]

---

[1] For more information on the Wallendas, see http://www.wallenda.com.

Perhaps I find Wallenda's story memorable because of my own vocation. I regularly walk a tightrope. It can be a thrilling experience, yet I live in fear of falling. I'm not an acrobat, though. I'm a professor of Bible and theology. In studying the Scriptures, sometimes I find a truth that does not seem to fit with another truth, and my mind tries to find a way to correlate the two without denying or diminishing either of them. How can I hold onto both of them at the same time? How can I keep from tipping too far in one direction or the other?

Bible students have wrestled with this problem for millennia. Sometimes our efforts leave us breathless at the edge of mystery. For instance, the Bible teaches plainly that there is only one God. But it also speaks of a Father, Son, and Spirit Who are God. Precise theological terminology helps us package the various strands of truth, and we end up with "three Persons in one Being." But we must admit that these words do not provide a full explanation. They only summarize a reality that we cannot understand this side of heaven and that we must accept by faith until then.

Not all biblical tensions are incomprehensible, however. Often there is a logical resolution, and it is found in noting different senses of a word or multiple aspects of a single truth. I believe that this is the case with the age-old tangle over law and grace. On the one hand, we have passages such as Romans 6:14: "For ye are not under the law, but under grace." This statement has been taken to imply that law and grace are mutually exclusive categories and that New Testament believers have no responsibility to the Old Testament law. Yet in the very next chapter Paul affirms that "the law is holy, and the commandment holy, and just, and good" (7:12), and later he speaks encouragingly of our fulfilling the law through love (13:8–10). We could easily produce a list of similar verses in tension.

Naturally one wonders whether the New Testament is for or against the law. This essay contends that in one sense the Christian is *not* under the law, but that in another sense he *is*. In addition to promoting a better understanding of Scripture, the goal is to help dispel contemporary confusion over "legalism" and Christian living.[2]

At the outset we need to acknowledge the difficulty of the issue. Jonathan Edwards wrote, "There is perhaps no part of divinity [theology] attended with so much intricacy, and wherein orthodox divines [theologians] do so much differ, as the stating [*sic*] the precise agreement and difference between the two dispensations of Moses and of Christ."[3] Consider who is speaking here—possibly the greatest intellect America has ever produced. When someone like him says that we are entering into the most debated theological topic, we would all do well to approach the discussion humbly and graciously. And Edwards does not stand alone in this assessment. Walter C. Kaiser Jr. quotes several modern scholars to the effect that Christian theology's master problem is determining the authority of the Old Testament for the New Testament believer.[4] Nor is this a new problem. The first theological council in the history of the church met over this very issue: "And certain men which came down from Judaea taught the brethren, and said, Except ye be circumcised after the manner of Moses, ye cannot be saved" (Acts 15:1).

---

[2]For a discussion of the definition of *legalism*, see Randy Jaeggli, *Love, Liberty, and Christian Conscience: Striking the Biblical Balance* (Greenville, SC: Bob Jones University Press, 2007).

[3]"An Humble Enquiry into the Rules of the Word of God, Concerning the Qualifications Requisite to a Complete Standing and Full Communion in the Visible Christian Church" [1749], ed. David B. Hall, in *The Works of Jonathan Edwards*, ed. Harry S. Stout (New Haven, CT: Yale University, 1994, 2002), 12:279.

[4]*Toward Rediscovering the Old Testament* (Grand Rapids: Zondervan, 1987), 13–14.

CRUCIAL DEFINITIONS

The long-standing debates should not discourage us from pursuing the matter further. On the contrary, the very difficulty of the subject should motivate us to study with all the more diligence. We can begin to make progress just by defining our terms carefully. What do we mean by *law* and *grace*? Or more importantly, what does the Bible mean by these words?

Law

Unfortunately, the English word *law* is not an exact fit for the biblical terms it translates. In common usage *law* focuses on a code of conduct laid down by an authority, and the word tends to create a negative reaction because it involves the restricting of behavior and the imposing of penalties for disobedience.[5] The biblical terms are broader and can be more positive. This is particularly the case with the Hebrew word *torah.* This noun actually means "instruction" or "direction," probably deriving from the verb *yarah*, "to teach, instruct." In connecting the two terms, the standard Hebrew lexicon suggests the idea of "stretching out the finger, or the hand, to point out a route."[6] But a word's breadth of usage is the final court of appeal, and it is significant that *torah* can refer to parental counsel (Prov. 1:8; 4:2; cf. 31:26) and instruction in narrative form (Ps. 78:1ff.; cf. Deut. 1:5).[7]

---

[5] Out of fourteen definitions for *law, The American Heritage Dictionary of the English Language*, 4th ed. (Boston: Houghton Mifflin, 2000) lists these first: "1. A rule of conduct or procedure established by custom, agreement, or authority. 2a. The body of rules and principles governing the affairs of a community and enforced by a political authority. b. The condition of social order and justice created by adherence to such a system." Interestingly, definition 9 confirms that this emphasis carries over into religious usage: "Law a. The body of principles or precepts held to express the divine will, especially as revealed in the Bible."

[6] Ludwig Koehler and Walter Baumgartner, *The Hebrew and Aramaic Lexicon of the Old Testament*, trans. M. E. J. Richardson (Leiden: Brill, 1999), 4:1710.

[7] See further Peter Enns, "Law of God," in *The New International Dictionary of Old Testament Theology and Exegesis*, ed. Willem A. VanGemeren (Grand Rapids: Zonder-

In most cases *torah* refers to divine commandments. Genesis 26:5 provides an example from the time of Abraham. Typically the commandments in view are those that Yahweh gave through Moses (Exod. 24:12), encompassing specific directives on multiple areas of life (Lev. 6:14; 14:2) or legal decisions based on them (Deut. 17:11), many of which involve legal, physical penalties. *Torah* was then used to identify collections of these commandments (Deut. 30:10) or the entire Mosaic Law—*the* Torah (1 Kings 2:3).

The New Testament word for *law, nomos,* usually refers to the Torah in some way. The word can mean "custom" or "principle" (Rom. 8:2) or "law" in a general sense (Rom. 3:27). But most of the time *nomos* has an Old Testament background, whether a specific commandment (Rom. 7:2), the Mosaic law as a whole (Acts 6:13), the Pentateuch (Luke 16:16), or the entire Old Testament (John 10:34).[8] Most important for our purposes, as Thomas R. Schreiner demonstrates, "Paul normally uses the word *law* [*nomos*] to refer to the commands of the Mosaic law."[9] We need to emphasize, however, that neither *torah* nor *nomos* inherently communicates the attitude with which the commandments are given, the motives for which they should be obeyed, or the nature of the relationship between the Lawgiver and the law-keeper. We must determine these matters by studying the covenants in which the commandments are given and the contexts in which they are discussed. We will have to deal with such questions as our study continues.

---

van, 1997), 4:897. My discussion of *torah* is based on the distinction between a word's meaning/sense and its referents. See Moisés Silva, *Biblical Words and Their Meaning: An Introduction to Lexical Semantics,* rev. ed. (Grand Rapids: Zondervan, 1994), 101–8.

[8] See further Frederick William Danker, ed., *A Greek English Lexicon of the New Testament and Other Early Christian Literature,* 3rd ed. (Chicago: University of Chicago, 2000), 677–78.

[9] *The Law and Its Fulfillment: A Pauline Theology of Law* (Grand Rapids: Baker, 1993), 39. Schreiner also shows (33–34) that *nomos* typically refers to the Mosaic law whether or not it is preceded by a definite article.

Grace

God's grace is commonly defined as His "undeserved favor." This is an adequate working definition, but here again we need to fine-tune our understanding based on the original languages. The Hebrew word family for grace, rooted in the verb *chanan*, certainly relates to the granting of favor. However, at times such favor comes in direct response to some positive action or quality. Between humans, for example, Joseph found favor with Potiphar because Potiphar was impressed with the divine prosperity Joseph enjoyed (Gen. 39:3–4). Negatively, a wife may no longer find favor from her husband because of some indecency (Deut. 24:1). Even in the divine-human relationship, God's favor comes to those who display loyalty and follow their parents' instruction (Prov. 3:4; cf. vv. 1–3). As just one sign of His goodness, God also shows favor to people who harden themselves against Him (Neh. 9:17, 31). But on the other hand, He may choose to withhold it from those who persist in sin (Jer. 16:13) while granting it to those who repent (Isa. 30:19).

So in the Old Testament, grace is not always unprompted. Rather, the point is simply that it is a *favor*—something God does not *have* to do, something that cannot be *required* of Him as an obligation or as a matter of justice. This concept appears most clearly in the adverb *chinnam*. Consider Exodus 21:2: "If thou buy an Hebrew servant, six years he shall serve: and in the seventh he shall go out free for nothing" (cf. v. 11; Gen. 29:15; Job 1:9). Here *chinnam* is translated "for nothing" and parallels the word *free*. Such references confirm the idea of grace as a *gift*, something given freely as opposed to something that can be purchased or demanded. And in a famous passage Yahweh asserts His sovereign right to determine how this favor is dispensed: "[I] will be gracious [*chanan*] to whom I will be gracious and will shew mercy on whom I will shew mercy" (Exod. 33:19).

The Greek word for grace, *charis*, largely parallels its Hebrew counterpart. For example, Acts 24:27 uses *charis* of a favor that Felix wanted to do for the Jews ("pleasure," KJV). In 1 Corinthians 16:3 *charis* refers to a monetary gift ("liberality," KJV). Of course, our main concern is God's grace. Here we find again that there may be conditions attached: He "giveth grace unto the humble" (James 4:6). But the New Testament strongly contrasts such divine favor with that which can be *earned* by human effort and therefore demanded. "Now to him that worketh is the reward not reckoned of grace, but of debt" (Rom. 4:4). "Therefore it is of faith, that it might be by grace" (Rom. 4:16). "And if by grace, then is it no more of works: otherwise grace is no more grace. But if it be of works, then is it no more grace: otherwise work is no more work" (Rom. 11:6).

Romans 3:24 provides a final example: "Being justified freely by his grace through the redemption that is in Christ Jesus." This verse emphasizes its point by using the synonymous expressions "freely" and "by his grace." The word translated "freely" (*dōrean*) appears in John 15:25 in a quotation from the Old Testament: "They hated me without a cause" (Ps. 35:19 or 69:4 or both). What is striking is that in Hebrew the phrase *without a cause* is the adverb *chinnam* we discussed earlier.

This, then, is the grace of God: what He does for man "without a cause"—without anything from us that would oblige Him to show us kindness. Or as one writer puts it, God's grace is His "uncoerced initiative and pervasive, extravagant demonstrations of care and favour."[10] These demonstrations are varied: salvation from sin (Eph. 2:8), spiritual growth (2 Pet. 3:18), endurance in trials (2 Cor. 12:9), special capacities for ministry (Rom. 12:6), and enabling to

---

[10]J. B. Green, "Grace," in *New Dictionary of Biblical Theology*, eds. T. Desmond Alexander and Brian S. Rosner (Downers Grove, IL: InterVarsity, 2000), 527.

minister diligently (1 Cor. 15:10) and abundantly (2 Cor. 9:8). But our topic is broader than these areas and encompasses them all. If in fact God has showered us with unmerited favor, what is our relationship to the many commandments in Scripture—specifically those in the Old Testament Torah?

2

COMPETING VIEWS

As we wrestle with the issue of law and grace, we will gain insight from considering how God's people have handled it throughout history. This exercise will identify the key passages to study, the interpretive questions to ask, and the alternatives proposed by orthodox scholars. We will concentrate on four especially influential views. The first two emphasize the similarities or continuities between the Testaments: Reformed theology and a subset known as theonomy. The other two positions are oriented toward the dissimilarities or discontinuities: dispensationalism and Lutheranism. The analyses below are necessarily simplified but should provide a sufficient working knowledge.[1] I will follow with a brief evaluation that will reinforce the importance of our discussion and clarify the path forward as we look at the Scriptures in more detail.

REFORMED THEOLOGY

The label *Reformed theology* technically describes one of the traditions that flowed from the Protestant Reformation of the sixteenth century—theology as developed particularly by John Calvin and his followers, different in significant ways from the Lutheran and Anabaptist wings of the Reformation.[2] Reformed theology is

---

[1]For more detailed summaries and further sources, see Wayne G. Strickland, ed., *Five Views on Law and Gospel* (Grand Rapids: Zondervan, 1999). Compare Donald G. Bloesch, *Freedom for Obedience: Evangelical Ethics in Contemporary Times* (San Francisco: Harper & Row, 1987), 106–25.

[2]For background on the Reformation, see Timothy George, *Theology of the Reformers* (Nashville: Broadman, 1988).

especially known for its emphasis on the sovereignty of God and the famous "five points of Calvinism." But more important for our purposes is another aspect of the Reformed tradition—covenant theology. This is a way of analyzing the overall theme and structure of the Bible.[3]

Covenant theology views the flow of Scripture in terms of two primary covenants. The first is typically called the covenant of works: the arrangement between God and Adam whereby God promised him eternal life on condition of perfect obedience. Adam broke this covenant by eating from the forbidden tree and cursed the entire race he represented to physical and spiritual death. In response God instituted a second covenant, the covenant of grace. This new arrangement did not set aside the covenant of works. Rather, it graciously provided for the fulfillment of the covenant of works through a Substitute, the Seed of the woman (Gen. 3:15)—Jesus Christ, the second Adam (Rom. 5:19). The benefits of this covenant are enjoyed by means of faith, resting in Christ's work on our behalf.

For covenant theologians, the covenant of grace covers the entire Bible from Genesis 3:15 (or at least 12:1) forward and constitutes the Bible's unifying message: redemption. The covenant of grace has been administered in different ways, however. During the period of "the law," God worked through a highly symbolic arrangement with the nation Israel. In the period of "the gospel," Jesus Christ finally came. His work fulfilled all the Israelite types and satisfied all the demands God had made of men. Now the covenant of grace has gone out in much greater clarity and power to all the nations. Nevertheless, covenant theologians emphasize the unity of the covenant of grace in all ages. In the words of the classic formulation of covenant theology, the English Puritans' West-

---

[3]For a standard contemporary defense of covenant theology, see O. Palmer Robertson, *The Christ of the Covenants* (Phillipsburg, NJ: Presbyterian & Reformed, 1980).

minster Confession (1646), "There are not therefore two covenants of grace, differing in substance, but one and the same, under various dispensations."[4]

Belief in the unity of the covenant of grace brings with it a great appreciation for the Old Testament and the ongoing use of its law. In an effort to work out the details, Reformed theology subdivides the Mosaic law into three categories that are accepted in various circles. First, the *moral* law expresses God's absolute religious and ethical demands. It is summarized in the Ten Commandments (Exod. 20:1–17; Deut. 5:1–22), the first four outlining man's duty to God and the other six delineating man's duty to his fellow man. Second, the *ceremonial* law spells out the specifics of *Israelite* religion, including instructions concerning the tabernacle, the sacrificial system, the priesthood, and the annual feasts—all of these rich in typology, visual prophecies of the Messiah and His work. Third, the *civil* (or judicial) law constitutes an application of the moral law to particular situations within national Israel.

We must now consider individually each category of law. Adapting the analysis of Lutheran theologian Philip Melanchthon, Calvin popularized three uses of the **moral** law that remain foundational to Reformed thinking. First is its *convicting* use. "While it shows God's righteousness, that is, the righteousness alone acceptable to God, it warns, informs, convicts, and last condemns, every man of his own unrighteousness."[5] Thus the sinner is cast on God's mercy in Christ as the only hope of acceptance with God (Rom. 3:19ff.). Second, the moral law has a *restraining* use in that its punishments curb wrongdoing and promote order in society (1 Tim. 1:9–10).[6]

---

[4] *Westminster Confession of Faith* (Glasgow: Free Presbyterian Publications, 1995), 7.6.

[5] John Calvin, *Institutes of the Christian Religion*, trans. Ford Lewis Battles, ed. John T. McNeill (Louisville: Westminster John Knox, 1960), 2.7.6.

[6] Ibid., 2.7.10–11.

The third use of the moral law is the most important and the one most useful for the Christian seeking to benefit from the Old Testament. We might call it the *guiding* use, whereby the moral law provides believers with a rule of life.

> Here is the best instrument for them to learn more thoroughly each day the nature of the Lord's will to which they aspire, and to confirm them in the understanding of it. . . . Again, because we need not only teaching but also exhortation, the servant of God will avail himself of this benefit of the law: by frequent meditation upon it to be aroused to obedience, be strengthened in it, and be drawn back from the slippery path of transgression.[7]

Consequently, Calvin and his successors go to great lengths to explore the implications of the Ten Commandments for Christian living. To help in this venture, Calvin proposed two guidelines. First, he urged that we pay attention to internal, not just external, righteousness (as Christ did in Matt. 5:28).[8] Second, "the commandments and prohibitions always contain more than is expressed in words." For instance, any stated reason given for a command will open up fresh applications about what pleases and displeases God. In addition, a prohibition implies an opposite positive duty and vice-versa.[9]

Armed with such principles, Reformed theologians emphasize the permanence of God's moral law in all ages. For example, though arguing that Jesus "simplified" the law with His emphasis on love for God and neighbor (Matt. 22:37–40), Willem A. VanGemeren asserts that "under both covenants, the Lord has one standard for ethics, namely holiness or wholeness of life. . . . The

---

[7]Ibid., 2.7.12.
[8]Ibid., 2.8.6–7.
[9]Ibid., 2.8.8.

Ten Commandments, as a summary of the moral law, are a guide in the imitation of God. By the Spirit the letter becomes alive and powerful within the hearts of the godly."[10]

The contemporary use of the **ceremonial** law is limited, since Hebrews emphatically teaches that the shadows of Israel's rituals have been abolished with the coming of Christ, the substance (e.g., Heb. 10:1ff.). The ceremonial law does have theological and devotional value, however, in illuminating our understanding of God's redemptive plan.

Finally, the **civil** law has been abolished too since it was so closely connected with the form that God's kingdom took in the nation of Israel (the "theocracy"), an arrangement no longer operative. However, the Puritans spoke of the "general equity" of the civil laws, referring to timeless principles that underlie the laws and that have relevance for all governments.[11] Debate over this last category leads us to consider a particular type of Reformed theology.

THEONOMY

The word *theonomy* means simply "the law of God." The distinctive of those who carry this label is the direct application of the Old Testament's civil laws to modern governments. However, their driving passion is Christ's lordship over every aspect of life—not just personal character, family relationships, and local church concerns. Thus, says the theonomist, the Christian must think scripturally about the sociopolitical realm. One key passage is Psalm 2, where Yahweh calls upon the rebellious kings of the earth to serve Him and submit to the Messiah (vv. 10–12). When one looks for biblical specifics on how governments should operate, most of the

---

[10] "The Law Is the Perfection of Righteousness in Jesus Christ: A Reformed Perspective," in *Five Views*, 36.

[11] *Westminster Confession*, 19.4.

revelation regards the nation Israel—a nation that was designed by God to be a model of righteousness to the other nations (Deut. 4:5–8). Though acknowledging ceremonial and cultural differences between the Testaments, theonomists argue that modern states are bound to follow Israel's civil laws unless Scripture clearly repeals those laws.

The Torah's legal penalties come to the fore here. Even the New Testament states that civil magistrates have been appointed by God and do not bear "the sword" in vain (Rom. 13:1–6). According to theonomists, this task of punishing evildoers should follow the lines of Old Testament law, meaning that capital punishment—at least as a maximum penalty—applies to a variety of offenses such as idolatry (Exod. 22:20), adultery (Deut. 22:22), incest (Lev. 20:11), homosexuality (Lev. 20:13), and even persistent disobedience to parents (Deut. 21:18–21).

The effort to use legal reform to influence governments in this direction is a key aspect in the platform of "Christian Reconstruction." This movement is closely associated with postmillennial eschatology, the viewpoint that Christ will return to earth after the church has enjoyed a golden age of transforming influence over the world. Until his death in 1995, Greg L. Bahnsen was probably the most articulate spokesman for these ideals. The following quotation typifies his teaching:

> The Christian's political standards and agenda must not be set by unregenerate pundits who wish to quarantine religious values (and thus the influence of Jesus Christ as recorded in the Scripture) from the decision-making process of those who set public policy. Theonomists equally repudiate the sacred/secular dichotomy of life. . . . Theonomists are committed to the transformation or reconstruction of every area of life, including the institutions

and affairs of the social-political realm, in accordance with the holy principles of God's revealed Word. . . . Christ is entitled to, and settles for, nothing less than immanent authority over all things, including the political potentates of this earth, "because he is Lord of lords and King of kings" (Rev. 17:14).[12]

DISPENSATIONALISM

At the opposite end of the spectrum is dispensationalism. The term *dispensation* translates the Greek *oikonomia*,[13] a word meaning "the stewardship or administration of a household" (e.g., Luke 16:2). Theologically it refers to a particular way in which God has administered His affairs in the world (e.g., Eph. 1:10). As was evident in the above quotations from the Westminster Confession, even covenant theologians believe that God has employed different dispensations in history. However, dispensationalism identifies and defines the dispensations differently.[14] It does not structure the Bible around a unifying covenant of grace. Rather, it views the dispensations as considerably separate divisions in God's program for establishing His kingdom on earth, in which different principles are stressed.

Traditionally, dispensationalists have held to seven dispensations: Innocence (from Creation to the Fall), Conscience (from the Fall to the Flood), Civil Government (from the Flood to Abraham), Promise (from Abraham to the Sinaitic covenant), Mosaic Law

---

[12]"The Theonomic Reformed Approach to Law and Gospel," in *Five Views*, 117–18. Bahnsen develops his position at length in *Theonomy in Christian Ethics*, 3rd ed. (Nacogdoches, TX: Covenant, 2002). Compare the writings of Rousas J. Rushdoony, especially *The Institutes of Biblical Law* (Phillipsburg, NJ: Presbyterian & Reformed, 1980).

[13]As has often been noted, this Greek word is the source of the English word *economy*.

[14]The standard contemporary defense of dispensationalism is Charles C. Ryrie, *Dispensationalism*, recently revised and expanded in a third edition (Chicago: Moody, 2007).

(from the Sinaitic covenant to the Cross or Pentecost), Grace or
the Church Age (from Pentecost to the Rapture or the Second
Coming), and the Millennium or the Kingdom (from the Second
Coming to the Great White Throne Judgment). However, not all
these divisions are at the core of dispensationalism. What is critical is the distinction between the period of the Mosaic law and the
period of grace—more specifically, the distinction between Israel
and the church as different bodies with different purposes and different administrative arrangements.

Naturally, dispensationalism sees a much greater dichotomy between law and grace than Reformed theology. Sometimes the dichotomy made has been almost total. Consider, for example, the
perspective of Lewis Sperry Chafer:

> The law is a system demanding human merit, while the
> injunctions addressed to the Christian under grace are un-
> related to human merit. Since the child of God is already
> accepted in the Beloved and stands forever in the merit of
> Christ, application of the merit system is both unreason-
> able and unscriptural. When the principles contained in
> the merit system reappear in the grace injunctions, it is al-
> ways with this vital change in character.[15]

Contemporary dispensational scholarship does not argue in quite
the same way as Chafer. For instance, Charles C. Ryrie's view

> distinguishes between a code of conduct and the com-
> mandments contained therein. The Mosaic Law was one
> of several codes of ethical conduct that God has given
> throughout human history. . . . The Mosaic code con-
> tained all the laws of the Law. And today we live under
> the law of Christ (Gal. 6:2) or the law of the Spirit of life

---

[15] *Systematic Theology* (Dallas: Dallas Seminary, 1948), 3:240.

in Christ (Rom. 8:2). This code contains the hundreds of specific commandments recorded in the New Testament.

The Mosaic Law was done away in its entirety as a code. It has been replaced by the law of Christ. The law of Christ contains some new commands (1 Tim. 4:4), some old ones (Rom. 13:9), and some revised ones (Rom. 13:4, with reference to capital punishment). All the laws of the Mosaic code have been abolished because the code has. Specific Mosaic commands that are part of the Christian code appear there not as a continuation of part of the Mosaic Law, or in order to be observed in some deeper sense, but as specifically incorporated into that code, and as such they are binding on believers today.[16]

Thus the general drift of dispensationalism is that a believer is not bound to an Old Testament law unless that law is repeated in the New Testament. However, dispensationalists may derive additional benefit from the law. For example, Wayne G. Strickland holds that both the Mosaic law and "the law of Christ" are "specific applications of God's eternal moral standard" (cf. Rom. 2:14–15). Consequently "the *principle* expressed in a Mosaic statute may still be preached in the church in the same sense as the fulfillment of the law of Christ furnishes fulfillment of the *essence* of the Mosaic Law."[17]

LUTHERANISM

Martin Luther's views on the law were foundational to his entire theology. These views are complex, however—some would even

---

[16] *Basic Theology: A Popular Systematic Guide to Understanding Biblical Truth* (Chicago: Moody, 1999), 351–52.

[17] "The Inauguration of the Law of Christ with the Gospel of Christ: A Dispensational View," in *Five Views*, 277–78 (emphasis added).

say ambiguous.[18] Given the Reformer's agonizing struggle to escape and then correct the works-salvation of Roman Catholicism, he naturally emphasized the distinction between "law" and "gospel." Luther defined law as the declaration of God's will that convicts man and threatens him with wrath. The gospel, on the other hand, is the declaration of God's mercy that comforts man and promises him forgiveness.

Though the Mosaic law is the dominant manifestation of law in Scripture, Luther did not limit law or gospel to a particular period or Testament. Rather, both principles run throughout the Bible, and every passage falls into one category or the other: "Whatever is Scripture is either law or gospel. One of the two must triumph: the law leads to despair, the gospel leads to salvation."[19] Making this distinction is critical both to interpreting the Bible and to resisting Satan's attacks.[20] The Formula of Concord (1576/1584) memorialized this concept for Lutheran churches: "We believe, teach, and confess that the distinction between law and Gospel is an especially glorious light that is to be maintained with great diligence in the church so that, according to St. Paul's admonition [2 Tim. 2:15], the Word of God may be divided rightly."[21]

Luther taught that the law continues to function in the believer as it does in the unbeliever—exposing our sin in order to draw us continually to Christ and dependence on Him. This is what the

---

[18]See David Wright, "The Ethical Use of the Old Testament in Luther and Calvin: A Comparison," *Scottish Journal of Theology* 36 (1983): 463–85.

[19]Martin Luther, "Heretics Provoke Theologian to Search Scriptures," trans. Theodore G. Tappert, in *Luther's Works*, ed. Helmut T. Lehmann (Philadelphia: Fortress, 1967), 54:111.

[20]See "Two Rules for Translating the Bible" and "Devil Upsets Distinction Between Law and Gospel" in ibid., 42–43, 105–7.

[21]*Formula of Concord*, 5.1, in *The Book of Concord: The Confessions of the Evangelical Lutheran Church*, trans. and ed. Theodore G. Tappert (Philadelphia: Fortress, 1959), 478.

Formula of Concord has in mind in its version of the "third use" of the law: "We believe, teach, and confess that the preaching of the law is to be diligently applied not only to unbelievers and the impenitent but also to people who are genuinely believing, truly converted, regenerated, and justified through faith."[22] But Luther also emphasized that God gave the Mosaic law to the Israelites, not to the Gentiles. As a result he makes very strong statements against the use of the Mosaic law today:

> If I were to accept Moses in one commandment, I would have to accept the entire Moses. Thus the consequence would be that if I accept Moses as master, then I must have myself circumcised, wash my clothes in the Jewish way, eat and drink and dress thus and so, and observe all that stuff. So, then, we will neither observe nor accept Moses. Moses is dead. His rule ended when Christ came. He is of no further service. . . . For not one little period in Moses pertains to us.[23]

Yet right in the middle of these comments, Luther makes a considerable qualification: "We will regard Moses as a teacher, but we will not regard him as our lawgiver—unless he agrees with both the New Testament and the natural law."[24] He goes on to explain three ways in which the Mosaic law remains helpful. First, it contains commandments that are part of God's "natural law" in every man (Rom. 2:14–15). The Christian is free to use other commandments as models for how to live today. Second, the Christian can

---

[22] *Formula*, 6.2, in *Book of Concord*, 480. See further Mark A. Seifrid, "Rightly Dividing the Word of Truth: An Introduction to the Distinction between Law and Gospel," *The Southern Baptist Journal of Theology* 10 (2006): 56–68.

[23] "How Christians Should Regard Moses," trans. E. Theodore Bachmann, in *Luther's Works*, ed. Helmut T. Lehmann (Philadelphia: Muhlenberg, 1960), 35:165–66.

[24] Ibid., 165.

still feed on Moses' messianic prophecies. Finally, Moses' writings also include biographies that serve as moral examples.[25]

The complexity increases as we turn to Luther's handling of the Ten Commandments in connection with his catechisms. He makes the statement that these commandments "forbid and teach what one must do and not do."[26] In dealing with the Sabbath, he asserts that "according to its literal, outward sense, this commandment does not concern us Christians." But then he offers a "Christian interpretation": "This, then is the plain meaning of this commandment: Since we observe holidays anyhow, we should devote their observance to learning God's Word."[27]

Responding to the tensions above, Douglas J. Moo has developed a modified Lutheran approach that provides a detailed synthesis of the biblical data on law and grace.[28] Definitions form his starting point:

> The New Testament use of the word "law" (*nomos*) is decisively conditioned by the Old Testament background and the Jewish milieu in which it was written. The word therefore almost always denotes not "law" in general, but the Mosaic Law, the *Torah* (*tôrâh*). As a result, the New Testament Law-"Gospel" tension is not, as in Luther, primarily static and theological, but historical. "Law" (*tôrâh*) came into history at a specific point in time (430 years after the promise, according to Gal. 3:17). In the New Testament,

[25] Ibid., 166–70.

[26] "Ten Sermons on the Catechism," trans. John W. Doberstein, in *The Works of Martin Luther*, ed. Helmut T. Lehmann (Philadelphia: Muhlenberg, 1959), 51:138.

[27] *The Large Catechism*, in *Book of Concord*, 376.

[28] "The Law of Christ as the Fulfillment of the Law of Moses: A Modified Lutheran View," in *Five Views*, 319–76. Compare Moo's "The Law of Moses or the Law of Christ," in *Continuity and Discontinuity: Perspectives on the Relationship Between the Old and New Testaments: Essays in Honor of S. Lewis Johnson*, ed. John S. Feinberg (Wheaton, IL: Crossway, 1988), 203–18.

therefore, Law and "Gospel" primarily denote, not two constant aspects of God's word to us, but two successive eras in salvation history.[29]

Reading the relevant texts in light of these definitions, Moo comes to this conclusion regarding the believer's relationship to the law:

> The entire Mosaic law comes to fulfillment in Christ, and this fulfillment means that this law is no longer a *direct and immediate* source of, or judge of, the conduct of God's people. Christian behavior, rather, is now guided directly by "the law of Christ." This "law" does not consist of legal prescriptions and ordinances, but of the teaching and example of Jesus and the apostles, the central demand of love, and the guiding influence of the indwelling Holy Spirit.[30]

This does not mean, however, that the Old Testament law has no continuing role in Christian living. For instance, "the detailed stipulations of the Mosaic law often reveal principles that are part of God's word to his people in both covenants, and believers continue to profit from what the law teaches in this respect."[31]

EVALUATING THE VIEWS

Space does not permit a detailed critique of the positions described above.[32] I will make some basic observations, however, that will focus our discussion. Regarding **Reformed theology**, I must express profound appreciation for its emphasis on the unity of God's plan of salvation and its Christ-centered interpretation of the Old Testament. However, I find the covenant-of-works/covenant-of-grace system difficult to uphold exegetically as a way to synthesize

---

[29] "Law of Christ," 322.

[30] Ibid., 343.

[31] Ibid., 376.

[32] For more developed evaluations, see the responses given after each essay in *Five Views*.

the progress of revelation. Even some Reformed theologians argue that the traditional approach is a bit simplistic and have offered more nuanced analyses.[33]

Similarly, I admire Reformed theologians as the ones who have worked the hardest to apply the Mosaic law legitimately to the Christian life. Nevertheless, I question their division of the law into moral, ceremonial, and civil categories. The Bible does make some commandments more important than others (e.g., Matt. 22:37–40) and also subordinates certain matters of worship to more fundamental moral/spiritual concerns (e.g., Mic. 6:6–8; Matt. 23:23). But it also emphasizes that the Mosaic law is an indivisible unity (e.g., Gal. 5:3; James 2:10–11).

Although the three proposed categories are reasonable, the Bible does not make these rigid distinctions, nor does it make such distinctions the basis for determining application. Here again, contemporary Reformed writers have critiqued their own tradition and have issued helpful correctives.[34] In fact, I once heard a Reformed Old Testament scholar argue that even the Ten Commandments cannot be equated exactly with "moral law," or else Christians would need to observe the Sabbath on Saturday instead of Sunday.[35]

---

[33]See, for example, Fred H. Klooster, "The Biblical Method of Salvation: A Case for Continuity," in *Continuity and Discontinuity*, 131–60. Compare Thomas Edward McComiskey, *The Covenants of Promise: A Theology of the Old Testament Covenants* (Grand Rapids: Baker, 1985).

[34]See Knox Chamblin, "The Law of Moses and the Law of Christ," in *Continuity and Discontinuity*, 181–202; Vern S. Poythress, *The Shadow of Christ in the Law of Moses* (Phillipsburg, NJ: Presbyterian & Reformed, 1991), 99–106. Compare the prerelease edition of John M. Frame, *The Doctrine of the Christian Life*, 199–203, available at http://reformedperspectives.org/newfiles/joh_frame/pt.frame.dcl.1.3.13.1.pdf.

[35]This was Bruce Waltke, in a seminar entitled "The Relationship of the Mosaic Covenant to the Christian Faith," held at Reformed Theological Seminary, Charlotte, NC. For a complete discussion of the Sabbath issue, see D. A. Carson, ed., *From Sabbath to Lord's Day: A Biblical, Historical, and Theological Investigation* (Grand Rapids: Zondervan, 1982).

Considering **theonomy** specifically, recognition is in order for the emphasis on the universal lordship of Christ, the authority of the Bible, and the ongoing value of the Old Testament. However, it is not clear in Scripture that Christ intends to exercise His lordship over civil governments through a direct use of Israel's laws. This certainly does not seem to be the attitude of the apostles to the Mosaic law at the Jerusalem Council (Acts 15), nor the response of Paul toward the incestuous man at Corinth (1 Cor. 5; 2 Cor. 2).

I concur with the many who argue that theonomy fails to give sufficient weight to Israel's status as a nation in a unique covenant with God.[36] In addition, identifying which laws are binding seems too arbitrary to be convincing. For instance, Vern Poythress discusses the inconsistencies that arise when theonomists dismiss Leviticus 19:19 as a ceremonial law that has been abrogated.[37]

What about the discontinuity views? Chafer's explanation is at best poorly worded, seemingly confusing *law* with *legalism*. Luther's analysis makes some valid points but likewise lacks clarity. Yet I find much to agree with in the contemporary expressions of **dispensationalism** and **Lutheranism** since I consider myself a moderate dispensationalist.[38] I also find it significant that after years

---

[36]For a Reformed response, see William S. Barker and W. Robert Godfrey, eds., *Theonomy: A Reformed Critique* (Grand Rapids: Zondervan, 1990). For a dispensational response, see H. Wayne House and Thomas Ice, eds., *Dominion Theology: Blessing or Curse?* (Portland, OR: Multnomah, 1988); compare Layton MacDonald Talbert, "The Theonomic Postmillennialism of Christian Reconstruction: A Contrast with Traditional Postmillennialism and a Premillennial Assessment" (PhD diss., Bob Jones University, 1992).

[37]*Shadow of Christ*, 316ff. Leviticus 19:19 says, "Ye shall keep my statutes. Thou shalt not let thy cattle gender with a diverse kind: thou shalt not sow thy field with mingled seed: neither shall a garment mingled of linen and woollen come upon thee."

[38]As stated on page 43 of Bob Jones University's 2007–8 *Seminary and Graduate Studies Catalog*, "The faculty's expository method is characterized by a moderate dispensationalism. This dispensationalism maintains the distinction between Israel and the Church, a recognition of both the literal and spiritual forms of the Kingdom of God and a pretribulational, premillennial approach to eschatology."

of studying the law in the New Testament, Frank Thielman—a Presbyterian—recently concluded that the New Testament's emphasis is on the discontinuity between the Mosaic law and the present age.[39] This makes perfect sense given the first-century need to explain the newness of the church in contrast with God's former arrangement with Israel.

WHY BOTHER?

If your mind is whirling among all the different views and subviews, now you understand what Edwards meant when he said that integrating the Testaments was the most difficult theological issue—and why I live on a tightrope! Since two millennia's worth of spilled ink has not brought God's people to a consensus, at this point you may be questioning even more whether it is necessary to keep discussing the issue of law and grace. Of course, the goal of understanding God's Word more clearly ought to be motivation enough. But a number of practical considerations also urge us to explore this subject further.

Several factors call for a renewed focus on the differences between law and grace. First, there are always extremes to guard against. For example, I once heard a speaker urging Christian parents to adopt Jewish betrothal customs in helping their children toward marriage. After all, this is what Jesus' own parents did! Second, like the Israelites we all tend to misinterpret God's commandments as a means of achieving acceptance before Him. Third, contemporary attacks on the gospel center on the law-grace issue.[40]

---

[39] *The Law and the New Testament: The Question of Continuity*, Companions to the New Testament (New York: Crossroad, 1999).

[40] I refer here to a variety of views known collectively as "the New Perspective on Paul." These views are based on the thesis that Second Temple Judaism did *not* teach salvation by obedience to the Mosaic law and that the Judaizers that Paul opposed did not either. Consequently, we must rethink our understanding of what Paul wrote regarding the law and justification. The New Perspective concludes that Paul was not contrasting human effort and divine grace in salvation. Rather, he was opposing the

However, we have a problem in the other direction to address. I don't get the impression that the average Christian today is trying to do *too much* with the Old Testament law. Quite the opposite: God's revelation in the Old Testament is often ignored, contributing to the unholiness of many who profess Christ. God's people need encouragement and instruction in what to do with the first three-quarters of their Bible, and it is here that discontinuity-oriented discussions tend to be deficient. I'm thankful that this appears to be changing.[41] I trust our study will show that the

---

misuse of the Mosaic law to limit salvation to the Jews. Thus Paul's focus is the inclusion of the Gentiles in the New Covenant community. This interpretation has led to redefinitions of justification. In the version popularized by N. T. Wright, justification is defined in terms of membership in the covenant community instead of in terms of the imputation of Christ's righteousness; see Wright's summary in *What Saint Paul Really Said: Was Saul of Tarsus the Real Founder of Christianity?* (Grand Rapids: Eerdmans, 1997). The New Perspective may help to sharpen our exegesis at points, but it is essentially an unorthodox position. Therefore I am not inclined to discuss it in this essay. Conservative scholars have gone to great lengths to demonstrate the problems with the New Perspective. Notable works include D. A. Carson, Peter T. O'Brien, and Mark Seifrid, eds., *Justification and Variegated Nomism*, 2 vols. (Grand Rapids: Baker, 2001, 2004); Thomas R. Schreiner, *The Law and Its Fulfillment: A Pauline Theology of Law* (Grand Rapids: Baker, 1993); and Frank Thielman, *Paul and the Law: A Contextual Approach* (Downers Grove, IL: InterVarsity, 1994). Sadly, however, the New Perspective has influenced how some conservative scholars handle the contemporary application of the law. See Elmer A. Martens, "Embracing the Law: A Biblical Theological Perspective," *Bulletin for Biblical Research* 2 (1992): 1–28. A later article by Martens is more helpful: "How Is the Christian to Construe Old Testament Law?" *Bulletin for Biblical Research* 12 (2002): 199–216.

[41] See, for example, J. Daniel Hays, "Applying the Old Testament Law Today," *Bibliotheca Sacra* 158 (2001): 21–35. Very striking is Dale S. Dewitt, *Dispensational Theology in America during the Twentieth Century* (Grand Rapids: Grace Bible College, 2002). Dewitt would actually be considered an ultra-dispensationalist since he argues that the church began with the ministry of Paul instead of at Pentecost. Nevertheless, he strongly encourages the contemporary application of the theological principles of the law (pp. 382–83): "The Old Testament law contains rich material for a total world and life view appropriate to a people of God. It is unnecessary to resort to legalism or law-imposition to restore the law's moral principles to the thinking and operations of the church; and it is certainly not workable to attempt an imperious and coercive theonomy. What is needed is a principled Pauline-like use of the law to guide our thinking about those aspects of life which it addresses in a theistic way: law, government, economics, dependent persons and minorities in a community, work and vocations, justice and mercy; for these, the Old Testament is richer than the New. Israel's institutions represent a revelational 'slice of life' by exhibiting one people of the ancient

dispensational distinction between Israel and the church does not necessitate a slighting of the Old Testament law or of the unity of God's purpose in human history.

A PATH FORWARD

The variety of positions on law and grace can be deceiving. We will make significant headway in our discussion if we recognize the common ground shared by the different views. First, all agree that our righteous standing before God is based only on the work of Christ and is appropriated only by faith. Second, no one is trying to import the entirety of the Mosaic law into the present age. Third, it does not contradict any system to argue that the ethical principles underlying the Mosaic law have abiding significance. In this regard, many of the differences are matters of *emphasis*, *degree*, and *methodology*. For instance, after emphasizing discontinuity the Lutheran Moo clarifies,

> I am not then, suggesting, that the essential "moral" *content* of the Mosaic law is not applicable to believers. On the "bottom line" question of what Christians are actually to *do*, I could well find myself in complete agreement with, say, a colleague who takes a traditional reformed approach to the Mosaic law. The difference would lie not in what Christians are to do but in how it is to be discovered.[42]

Yet when responding to Strickland's dispensational position, Moo states, "I *generally* agree with almost all of Strickland's broad theological conclusions as well as with most of his specific exegetical

---

world as a sample of God's revealed moral will; the values of moral life found there may be transferred across revelational, temporal and cultural boundaries, much in the way Paul does with his own use of the law." Another helpful feature of Dewitt's work is his detailed critique (pp. 257ff.) of the novel views of Daniel P. Fuller, expressed in *Gospel and Law: Contrast or Continuum? The Hermeneutics of Dispensationalism and Covenant Theology* (Grand Rapids: Eerdmans, 1980).

[42] "Law of Christ," 376.

and theological arguments." Moo's disagreements relate to "tone" and "balance."[43] Not surprisingly, recent years have produced positions that do not fit comfortably in any camp because they incorporate emphases of various views. Examples include the writings of David A. Dorsey,[44] Walter C. Kaiser Jr.,[45] Joe M. Sprinkle,[46] and Christopher J. H. Wright.[47] The law-grace issue has also played a part in the development of entire theological systems that represent mediating positions between dispensationalism and covenant theology.[48]

All these factors suggest that we are dealing with a *both-and*, not an *either-or*, situation. We will find this suggestion confirmed as we look more closely at selected passages that represent the Scriptures' breadth of teaching. First we will see several ways in which we are *not* under the law. Then we will consider how the law nevertheless continues to function in the Christian life.

---

[43]Ibid., 309, 315.

[44]See "The Law of Moses and the Christian: A Compromise," *Journal of the Evangelical Theological Society* 34 (1991): 321–34; expanded in "The Use of the OT Law in the Christian Life: A Theocentric Approach," *Evangelical Journal* 17 (1999): 1–18.

[45]See "The Law as God's Gracious Guidance for the Promotion of Holiness," in *Five Views*, 177–99; *Toward Rediscovering*, 147–66; and *Toward Old Testament Ethics* (Grand Rapids: Zondervan, 1983).

[46]See *Biblical Law and Its Relevance: A Christian Understanding and Ethical Application for Today of the Mosaic Regulations* (Lanham, MD: University Press of America, 2006).

[47]See Wright's combination of his previous works in *Old Testament Ethics for the People of God* (Downers Grove, IL: InterVarsity, 2004).

[48]See Craig A. Blaising and Darrell L. Bock, *Progressive Dispensationalism* (Grand Rapids: Baker, 1993); Tom Wells and Fred Zaspel, *New Covenant Theology* (Frederick, MD: New Covenant, 2002).

3

WE ARE NOT UNDER THE LAW

A well-known hymn begins with "Free from the law, O happy condition."[1] Though this idea is easily abused, the New Testament does encourage us to rejoice that the Mosaic Law does not have direct authority over us. We will discuss key passages on this topic in three interrelated categories. Christians are not under the law (1) as a covenantal code, (2) as a way of salvation, or (3) as a general emphasis in our relationship with God.

NOT UNDER THE LAW AS A COVENANTAL CODE

One of our basic principles of biblical interpretation is interpreting in light of historical background. When reading a passage, we must always ask who wrote it, to whom, in what circumstances, and for what purpose. These are not merely academic questions. As Grant R. Osborne writes, studying the historical background "draws us out of our twentieth-century perspective [twenty-first!] and makes us aware of the ancient situation behind the text."[2] This exercise will guard us from misapplying a text to circumstances that are significantly different from those of the original audience. So before we can understand how the law relates to us, we must consider how it related to its original recipients.

---

[1] Philip P. Bliss, "Once for All."

[2] *The Hermeneutical Spiral: A Comprehensive Introduction to Biblical Interpretation* (Downers Grove: InterVarsity, 1991), 20.

Israel

As we read the law in its historical context, we note several features. First, it was given to ethnic Israelites. Yahweh addresses the Torah to "the house of Jacob" and "the children of Israel" (Exod. 19:3), whom He had physically delivered from slavery in Egypt (Exod. 19:4; 20:2). When He issues a "second edition" of the Torah forty years later, again the recipients are descendants of Abraham, Isaac, and Jacob who are preparing to conquer the land of Canaan (Deut. 1:8). Second, the Torah contains a myriad of directives highly specific to this ethnic/national entity. It addresses elements of ancient Near East culture (e.g., roof parapets, Deut. 22:8). It organizes a governmental structure tied to a particular geographic setting (e.g., the cities of refuge, Deut. 19). More importantly, it establishes an elaborate system of worship involving animal sacrifices, to be conducted at a centrally located building, centered on a Sabbath on the seventh day of each week (e.g., Exod. 25–31; Deut. 12).

Third, the Torah formed part of a covenant that God made with national Israel, known as the Mosaic or Sinaitic covenant (Exod. 19–24). As we explore the nature of this covenant, we immediately find ourselves on another tightrope. On the one hand, the Mosaic covenant was founded on God's grace. Before stating a single commandment, Yahweh issues a reminder: "Ye have seen what I did unto the Egyptians, and how I bare you on eagles' wings, and brought you unto myself" (19:4). God had already shown favor to the Israelites by delivering them from their bondage to the Egyptians. This disposition was secured by His free choice to love these people and by His prior covenant with their patriarchs (Deut. 7:6–8; cf. Exod. 2:23–25; 6:1–8). Obedience to the Torah was intended to be a response of gratitude for the privilege of being Yahweh's people and experiencing His loving intervention on their behalf.

We see the same truth at the beginning of the Ten Commandments: "I am the Lord thy God, which have brought thee out of the land of Egypt, out of the house of bondage. Thou shalt have no other gods before me" (Exod. 20:2–3). Notice that Yahweh identifies Himself as the Israelites' God already, before giving the commands and as an implied reason for keeping them. Another passage along these lines is Moses' stirring exhortation in Deuteronomy 4:32–40. Other manifestations of grace in the Mosaic covenant include the opportunity for obtaining atonement and forgiveness through the sacrificial system (e.g., Lev. 4:20) and the classic proclamation of Yahweh's character in Exodus 34:6–7. At least some Israelites internalized the truths above and lived in awe that the God of heaven had chosen to work in their lives and communicate His will to them (Ps. 147:19–20). In fact, they came to view His Torah as a source of joy: "O how love I thy law! it is my meditation all the day. . . . Thy law is my delight" (Ps. 119:97, 174).

But we must come to the other side. Despite its graciousness, the Mosaic covenant was conditional in nature. It involved human responsibilities that entailed radical consequences. In fact, right after the reminder about the Exodus in Exodus 19:4, Yahweh says, "Now therefore, *if* ye will obey my voice indeed, and keep my covenant, *then* ye shall be a peculiar treasure unto me above all people" (v. 5, emphasis added). The covenant was something that had to be kept. Conversely, it could be broken (Deut. 31:16). But it could also be renewed (e.g., Exod. 34). Further highlighting conditionality, the Pentateuch ends with long lists of curses and blessings that would ensue based on Israel's response to the Torah (Deut. 27–28; cf. Lev. 26). Through disobedience, individual generations of Israelites could forfeit their personal enjoyment of and participation in

God's program for the nation as a whole. It was quite possible to be an Israelite but not be in covenant with Yahweh.

The Church

When we come to New Testament descriptions of God's relationship with the church, we find considerably different arrangements. The church is a multiethnic, multinational body (Gal. 3:28) that is spread throughout the earth (1 Cor. 1:2; 1 Pet. 1:1). Therefore its members live under various governments (1 Pet. 2:13–14) and worship in various locales (e.g., Phil. 1:1; 1 Thess. 1:1). They gather for worship on the first day of the week, not the last (Acts 20:7; 1 Cor. 16:2). Amazingly, believers actually form God's temple today, both corporately (1 Cor. 3:6–7) and individually (1 Cor. 6:19).

Furthermore, we participate not in the Mosaic covenant but the New Covenant (2 Cor. 3:6–18), which is unbreakable (Heb. 8:6–13). Though obedience and disobedience still have consequences (e.g., Heb. 12:5–7), every true believer is assured that he will not lose his position in God's family (John 10:28–29; Rom. 8:33–39). Sin hinders our fellowship with God and must be confessed (1 John 1:9), but there is no such thing as a Christian who is not in a covenant relationship with God. These simple yet profound differences between Israel and the church demonstrate that we do not and cannot relate to the law in the same way the Israelites did.

But the New Testament is more emphatic than that. It specifically abrogates a number of the commandments in the Torah (e.g., circumcision, Gal. 5:2, 6; food laws, Mark 7:19, cf. Acts 10:9–16; the sacrificial system, Heb. 8–10; the holy days, Col. 2:16). Most significant is the declaration of the apostles and elders at the Jerusalem Council (Acts 15). This council convened to consider whether Gentiles had to submit to the Jewish covenant sign of circumcision in order to be saved (v. 1) and to the Mosaic law as a whole (v. 5). Regarding circumcision, two arguments won the day. First, Peter, Paul, and Barnabas recounted how Gentiles had received the Spirit without circumcision (vv. 7–12). Second, James asserted that the conversion of Gentiles as Gentiles (i.e., uncircumcised) was in keeping with the prophecy of Amos 9:11–12 (vv. 13–19). The church leaders concurred with James that they should not "trouble" the Gentiles with circumcision (v. 19).

Nevertheless, they still had to deal with the practical problems raised by the growing interaction between Jews and Gentiles. In this regard the council urged Gentile believers to avoid four activities: "Abstain from meats offered to idols, and from blood, and from things strangled, and from fornication" (v. 29). Commentators debate over the reasoning behind the items chosen for this list, especially the difference between "fornication" (Greek *porneia*) and the other three.[3] Whatever the case, the list cannot be an exhaustive catalog of Mosaic commands that remain binding. James must be assuming basic ethical standards that transcend the dispensations. For example, he does not mention the Old Testament's prohibition of stealing, which Paul views as in force today (Rom. 13:8–10).

But the most important point is that the apostles recognized a dramatic difference between Old and New Testament times and concluded that the Mosaic law does not function as a covenantal code for the church. Instead they analyzed their situation and called for selective observance. In their case the main concern was evidently

---

[3]For example, F. F. Bruce says that *porneia* "may be used here in a more specialized sense, of marriage within degrees of blood relationship or affinity forbidden by the legislation of Lev. 18:6–18. . . . Ordinary fornication, like ordinary idol-worship, was ruled out by the most elementary principles of Christian instruction." *The Book of the Acts*, rev. ed., The New International Commentary on the New Testament (Grand Rapids: Eerdmans, 1988), 299.

respect for strong Jewish sensitivities, in order to promote unity between Jewish and Gentile believers and maintain a testimony before Jewish unbelievers.[4]

NOT UNDER THE LAW AS A WAY OF SALVATION

At this juncture we need to broaden our discussion to ask *why* God effected the great change between Old and New Testament. Here we enter into the most complex aspect of our topic: the relation of the Mosaic law to the doctrine of salvation. First we will consider how the law operated in the lives of individual Israelites. Next we will see how this affects God's overall program of salvation in human history. Then we will have to answer some important questions that naturally arise from the discussion.

The Law and Salvation on the Individual Level

As we ask how the law and salvation relate in the salvation of individuals, we must explore further the nature of the Mosaic covenant. Then we can reflect on the experience of an Israelite living under that covenant.

The Necessity of Obedience

As we saw above, the Mosaic covenant involved a tension between graciousness and conditionality. To begin with, the covenant relationship was a divine gift, not something Israel earned through self-effort. We can highlight this truth with a New Testament verse that has often been misinterpreted. John 1:17 says, "For the law was given by Moses, but grace and truth came by Jesus Christ." Notice two facts about this verse. First, the conjunction *but* appears in italics in King James Version, indicating that the

---

[4]I say "evidently" because of the difficulties of explaining the four prohibitions and also because of the variety of interpretations possible for Acts 15:21 ("For Moses of old time hath in every city them that preach him, being read in the synagogues every sabbath day"). Compare Bruce, 296, with John B. Polhill, *Acts*, vol. 26 of The New American Commentary (Nashville: Broadman, 1992), 332.

translators of the inserted the word. Whether John intends the strong contrast conveyed by *but* can be determined only by the context, and it is here that we come to our second fact: verse 17 begins with *for*, suggesting that this verse is a reason or explanation for a previous assertion. This leads us to consider verse 16: "And of his [Jesus Christ's] fulness have all we received, and grace for grace." The term translated "for" here (*anti*) means "instead of" or "in exchange for."

With this in mind, the connection between verses 16 and 17 seems to be as follows: "We have all been blessed from Jesus' abundance with a grace that replaces earlier grace—because the law was given through Moses; grace and truth came into full realization through Jesus Christ." In other words, the law was a previous demonstration of grace; it is not contrary to grace.[5] Note also that John is speaking of both grace *and* truth. If we don't see here some measure of continuity between Moses and Jesus, we cast doubt on the very truthfulness of the revelation God gave through Moses.[6]

Nevertheless, John clearly views the incarnation as superior to the Mosaic law. Why is it superior? One reason is that the Mosaic covenant was conditional. Consider this key verse: "Ye shall therefore keep my statutes, and my judgments: which if a man do, he shall live in them: I am the Lord" (Lev. 18:5; cited in Ezek. 20:11, 13, 21; Neh. 9:29; Luke 10:28; Rom. 10:5; Gal. 3:12). Given the Bible's overall message, this verse cannot be teaching a salvation by works under the Mosaic covenant. Rather, "life" refers to a long,

---

[5]See further D. A. Carson, *The Gospel According to John*, The Pillar New Testament Commentary (Grand Rapids: Eerdmans, 1991), 132–34; Andreas J. Köstenberger, *John*, Baker Exegetical Commentary on the New Testament (Grand Rapids: Baker, 2004), 46–48.

[6]See further Joe M. Sprinkle, *Biblical Law and Its Relevance: A Christian Understanding and Ethical Application for Today of the Mosaic Regulations* (Lanham, MD: University Press of America, 2006), 29–40.

prosperous, and happy physical life in the Promised Land.[7] This becomes clear from our verse's context. Leviticus 18 catalogs over twenty prohibited sexual activities that were prevalent among the Egyptians and the Canaanites (v. 3). After going through the distasteful list, the Lord explains that His intent is to spare the Israelites from the kind of destruction the inhabitants of Canaan were about to suffer for their wickedness: "That the land spue not you out also, when ye defile it, as it spued out the nations that *were* before you" (v. 28). So the chapter's concern is physical protection and blessing.

This concern dominates the Pentateuch. For instance, Deuteronomy 5:33 says, "Ye shall walk in all the ways which the Lord your God hath commanded you, that ye may live, and that it may be well with you, and that ye may prolong your days in the land which ye shall possess." Likewise Deuteronomy 28 predicts that an obedient Israel could expect fertility, rain, agricultural fruitfulness, military victory, and international renown (vv. 1–14). Conversely, disobedience would bring drought, plague, disease, defeat, and humiliating exile (vv. 15–68). This emphasis on reward and retribution pervades the historical books (especially Chronicles) and forms the essence of the message of the prophets. Yahweh was absolutely committed to the descendants of Abraham as a whole. Nevertheless each generation of Israelites maintained its place in the covenant through obedience to the law.[8]

---

[7]So Gordon J. Wenham, *The Book of Leviticus*, The New International Commentary on the Old Testament (Grand Rapids: Eerdmans, 1979), 253, and many other commentators.

[8]Thomas Edward McComiskey expresses the tension this way: "The function of the law was not to grant the [Abrahamic] inheritance but to preserve and protect the people for the inheritance. . . . Obedience to the law prevented the dissolution of the entire nation at the hand of an angry God. It thereby insured the continuation of the nation and thus perpetuated the promise." *The Covenants of Promise: A Theology of the Old Testament Covenants* (Grand Rapids: Baker, 1985), 75.

With this background in mind, we can understand why Paul quoted Leviticus 18:5 in combating "Judaizers" who were attempting to impose the law as a requirement for salvation. In Galatians 3:10–12 he writes:

> For as many as are of the works of the law are under the curse: for it is written, Cursed is every one that continueth not in all things which are written in the book of the law to do them [Deut. 27:26]. But that no man is justified by the law in the sight of God, it is evident: for, The just shall live by faith [Hab. 2:4]. And the law is not of faith: but, The man that doeth them shall live in them [Lev. 18:5].

Paul's point is that the Mosaic covenant emphasized "doing." You had to obey in order to stay in the covenant and perhaps even to survive at all. The covenant was heavily contingent on human obedience, and this differs from a relationship based on faith alone.[9]

The Impossibility of Obedience

Now put yourself in the shoes of someone under the Mosaic covenant. You are humbled that God has graciously chosen you to be one of His special people and to receive the revelation of His will. On the other hand you are told that to maintain this relationship

---

[9]See the comments on Romans 10:5's use of Leviticus 18:5 in Douglas J. Moo, *The Epistle to the Romans*, The New International Commentary on the New Testament (Grand Rapids: Eerdmans, 1996), 645–48. Commentators have suggested other ways to understand Leviticus 18:5 in Paul's theology. For example, Reformed writers tend to speak of a hypothetical offer of salvation by works in the Mosaic covenant; see Thomas R. Schreiner, *Romans*, Baker Exegetical Commentary on the New Testament (Grand Rapids: Baker, 1998), 550–56. I believe this is going too far, since the Mosaic covenant dealt with physical blessing, not eternal life. However, there is a connection between the two, as I will suggest. Even less convincing is the idea that Leviticus 18:5 focuses on obedience as the evidence of faith and is analogous to sanctification (Walter C. Kaiser Jr., "Leviticus 18:5 and Paul: Do This and You Shall Live (Eternally?)," *Journal of the Evangelical Theological Society* 14 [1971]: 19–28). This explanation misses the contrast that Paul is making between obedience and faith—particularly in Galatians 3:12, a verse that Kaiser does not address.

and enjoy its blessings, you must obey the law. So you set out on this path enthusiastically.

But wherever you look, you are faced with discouraging facts. If you look at the law, you are overwhelmed with its detailed legislation. If you look at your nation's history, you find a depressing litany of failure after failure. Worst of all, if you look at your own heart, you grieve over your lack of desire and your carnality. Your anxiety grows as you realize that the law addresses the inner man. Deuteronomy 6:5 commands you to love Yahweh with all your heart, being, and strength. Deuteronomy 10:16 tells you to circumcise the foreskin of your heart. As if that weren't enough, one day you run across Deuteronomy 29:4: "The LORD hath not given you an heart to perceive, and eyes to see, and ears to hear."

At last you throw up your hands in despair and are tempted to blame God for your struggles. Then you are paralyzed with a new thought: if you can't obey enough to attain the earthly blessings of the Mosaic covenant, what hope do you possibly have for *eternal* life? Had you been living in the intertestamental period or later, your angst would have been even greater because religious authorities began teaching that law-keeping was, in fact, a condition for eternal life. For example, according to the tradition enshrined in the Aramaic Targum (paraphrase) of Onqelos (ca. AD 200), Leviticus 18:5 means the following: "You should observe My ordinances and (My) laws, which, if a person practices them, he will live through them *in the future world*; I am the Lord."[10]

---

[10]Bernard Grossfeld, trans., *The Targum Onqelos to Leviticus*, in *The Aramaic Bible*, eds. Kevin Cathcart, Michael Maher, and Martin McNamara (Wilmington, DE: Michael Glazier, 1988), 8:37. A medieval Targum expands the verse further: "And you shall observe my statutes and my ordinances, by keeping which a man shall live *in eternal life, and his portion shall be with the righteous.*" Michael Maher, trans., *Targum Pseudo-Jonathan: Leviticus*, in *The Aramaic Bible*, eds. Kevin Cathcart, Michael Maher, and Martin McNamara (Collegeville, MN: Liturgical, 1994), 3:173.

This dynamic is what lies behind the New Testament's "negative" statements regarding the law. It seems to be Peter's thinking when he told the Jerusalem Council, "Now therefore why tempt ye God, to put a yoke upon the neck of the disciples, which neither our fathers nor we were able to bear?" (Acts 15:10; cf. 13:39). In other words, "None of us Jews has been able to keep this law! How in the world can we impose it on Gentiles as a condition for justification?"[11]

Paul's epistles give the theological explanation for Peter's assessment: the problem is man's inability to keep the law. We see this in a verse quoted earlier, Galatians 3:10: "For as many as are of the works of the law are under the curse: for it is written, Cursed is every one that continueth not in all things which are written in the book of the law to do them." Thomas R. Schreiner helpfully presents this verse in the form of a syllogism:

> Those who do not keep everything written in the law are cursed (3:10*b*).
>
> No one keeps everything written in the law (implicit premise).
>
> Therefore, those who rely on the works of the law for salvation are cursed (3:10*a*).[12]

This reasoning is developed at length in Romans 1–3. Paul also presents a corollary to the human problem: the law could not enable man to obey; it had no life-giving power. Galatians 3:20–21 says that "if there had been a law given which could have given life, verily righteousness should have been by the law." Romans 8:3

---

[11] See Polhill, 327.

[12] *The Law and Its Fulfillment: A Pauline Theology of Law* (Grand Rapids: Baker, 1993), 44. Schreiner has an entire chapter (41–71) defending with detailed exegesis the thrust of the argument above, including a study of the phrase *works of law* and a refutation of aberrant interpretations.

summarizes our point in speaking of "what the law could not do, in that it was weak through the flesh."

The Law and Salvation on the Historical Level

Our next question is obvious: why did God require of the Israelites an obedience they could not offer? In answering, we finally arrive at the function the law plays in God's overall program for providing salvation and the closing of the historical period devoted to this function.

The Function of the Law

As you may have deduced from the discussion above, Paul's epistles to the Romans and the Galatians form the focal point of the New Testament discussion regarding the law. These letters do not provide a comprehensive discussion of all the law's functions. Rather, they focus on the law's function with reference to sin and salvation. To begin with, the law identifies sin by specifying what is and what is not God's will, and thus it provides legal grounds for accusing people of violations. This is the thrust of passages such as Romans 3:19–20, 4:15, and 5:13. But Paul makes an even stronger point in Romans 5:20: "The law entered, that the offence might abound" or "The Law came in so that the transgression would increase" (NASB). This is the opposite of what we would naturally think. It seems that the law would help people sin less, but in reality the law contributes to the development of more sin.

Paul explains himself more in Romans 7:7–13. Here he emphasizes that the law itself is good (v. 12). However, when the law confronts a man with its specific commandments, his sinful nature is aroused to do more evil because it hates being told what to do. Thus, rather than leading to life, the law results in death. Verse 13 states God's intent for this maddening experience: "That sin by the commandment might become exceeding sinful." The law becomes the means by which sin multiplies and its heinousness is manifested.

The connection between the law and sin is so close that 1 Corinthians 15:56 says, "The strength of sin is the law." Thus to be under the dominion of the law effectively means that a person is under the dominion of sin. This is the background of Paul's famous declaration in Romans 6:14. The second half of the verse presents the reason for the first half: "For sin shall not have dominion over you: for ye are not under the law, but under grace." In other words, if the law dominates a person's relationship to God, it only increases sin's hold on him. If God's grace in Christ dominates, however, one is freed from the tyranny of sin.

The End of the Law

We have more to say about Romans 6:14, though. Paul is not dealing here with the difference between any person's life before and after conversion—under the law, and then under grace. The last time he mentioned "the law" was in 5:20, where it is a force that "entered" human history at a certain point and resulted in the reign of sin. At present, however, grace reigns (5:21). Chapter 6 then has to deal with the question of whether such an emphasis on grace results in more sin (v. 1). Paul gives an extended negative answer by teaching that union with Christ brings victory over sin (vv. 2–13). Then his comment in verse 14 harks back to chapter 5's discussion of "the law" and "grace" as historical periods dominated by these forces. Moo explains,

> That the law is so suddenly brought onto the scene at the end of this paragraph reveals the extent to which Paul's presentation of his gospel in this letter never moves too far from the salvation-historical question of Old Covenant and New, Jew and Gentile. . . . "Under the law," then, is

another way of characterizing "the old realm." . . . To be "under the law" is to be subject to the constraining and sin-strengthening regime of the old age; to be "under grace" is to be subject to the new age in which freedom from the power of sin is available.[13]

Other passages make the same point as Romans 6:14. Here we might include Romans 10:4, "For Christ is the end of the law for righteousness to every one that believeth." The word translated "end" here (*telos*) may imply the idea of an intended goal but normally means termination.[14] In what sense, then, has Christ terminated the Mosaic law? To answer this question, we must consider verses 3 and 4 together: "For they [the Israelites] being ignorant of God's righteousness, and going about to establish their own righteousness, have not submitted themselves unto the righteousness of God. For Christ *is* the end of the law for righteousness to every one that believeth." Thus verse 4 responds to the Jews' efforts to achieve a right standing before God through personal obedience to the law.

The point may be simply that for those who believe the gospel, Christ ends their *wrong use* of the law to attain righteousness.[15] On the other hand, "the law" may again be describing the Mosaic Law as a historical phase in God's program of salvation: "The Jews' pursuit of a righteousness of their own, based on the law, is wrong because Christ has brought the law to its culmination and thereby made righteousness available to everyone who believes."[16]

---

[13]*Romans*, 387–89. So also Schreiner, *Romans*, 326, and Robert H. Mounce, *Romans*, vol. 27 of The New American Commentary (Nashville: Broadman & Holman, 1995), 154–55.

[14]For the data, see Schreiner, *Romans*, 545–46.

[15]Ibid., 545–48. So also Mounce, 207–8, and Leon Morris, *The Epistle to the Romans*, The Pillar New Testament Commentary (Grand Rapids: Eerdmans, 1988), 379–81.

[16]Moo, *Romans*, 636.

Paul is definitely speaking of the law as a historical phase in Galatians 3–4. In 3:15–18 the apostle explains that the Mosaic law was added 430 years after the Abrahamic covenant and cannot alter this covenant's focus on God's promise and the response of simple faith. This leads to the question "Why the Mosaic law?" Following is a portion of Paul's extended answer (vv. 19–25), with some interpretive comments:

> It [the law] was added because of transgressions [probably meaning to increase sin; cf. Rom. 5:20], till the seed [Christ; Gal. 3:16] should come to whom the promise was made; and it was ordained by angels in the hand of a mediator. Now a mediator is not a mediator of one, but God is one [the point being that the Abrahamic covenant is superior to the Mosaic because the former is unmediated and unilateral]. Is the law then against the promises of God? God forbid: for if there had been a law given which could have given life, verily righteousness should have been by the law. But the scripture hath concluded all under sin, that the promise by faith of [in] Jesus Christ might be given to them that believe. But before faith [literally "*the* faith," referring to the historical arrival of Christ as the basis for justification by faith] came, we were kept under the law [like prisoners being watched by a warden], shut up unto the faith which should afterwards be revealed. Wherefore the law was our schoolmaster [Greek *paidagōgos*, a custodian who supervised young boys until they arrived at maturity] to bring us unto Christ, that we might be justified by faith. [More simply, "The law was our custodian until Christ." "To bring us" is not in the Greek text; the preposition translated "unto" (*eis*) has the temporal force of "until."] But after that faith is come [now that

the faith, i.e., Christ, has come], we are no longer under a schoolmaster.[17]

Paul's main point is clear: the Mosaic law was a temporary measure whose legal jurisdiction ended when Christ came (cf. Luke 16:16). This teaching continues into Galatians 4, which announces that the period of childhood is over and the time of adulthood has arrived. Consequently Paul urges the Galatians not to be pressured into a re-submission to Mosaic holy days (v. 10).

One key passage remains: 2 Corinthians 3. Here Paul presents a series of contrasts between the New Covenant that he ministers and the Old Covenant that Moses ministered. Moses gave commandments on stone that "killed" the Israelites; in the New Covenant the Spirit gives people life (vv. 6–8). The Mosaic covenant was a ministry of condemnation; the New Covenant is a ministry of righteousness (vv. 9–10). The Mosaic covenant fades away; the New Covenant is permanent (v. 11). The Mosaic covenant involved obscurity, whereas in the New Covenant Paul speaks with great freedom (vv. 12–13). Finally, the Old Covenant could not remove spiritual blindness, but in the New Covenant the Holy Spirit illumines people and transforms them into the image of Christ (vv. 14–18).

Clarifications Regarding the Law and Salvation

Let's summarize what we have seen about the law's role in God's program of salvation. Yahweh graciously chose the nation Israel as His special people and entered into a covenant with them. But to stay in this covenant and enjoy a prosperous life in the Promised

---

[17]For exegetical details, see Ronald Y. K. Fung, *The Epistle to the Galatians*, The New International Commentary on the New Testament (Grand Rapids: Eerdmans, 1988), 158–70; Timothy George, *Galatians*, vol. 30 of The New American Commentary (Nashville: Broadman & Holman, 1994), 250–70. Compare Schreiner, *Law and Its Fulfillment*, 77–80, 124–29.

Land, the Israelites had to obey the covenant's many laws. They found this obedience impossible, however. This situation should have driven sensitive Israelites to realize the even more impossible task of earning eternal life. God actually gave the Israelites the law to expose and increase sin. Thus the impossibility of works salvation would be evident, and the stage would be set for the coming of Jesus Christ to provide justification by faith. Once Christ came, the Mosaic law's domination ended. By this time, however, the Jews had begun to view the law as a means of earning eternal life. This idea infiltrated the New Testament church, leading to Paul's teaching on the true function and historical end of the law. He showed that compared to the New Covenant, the Mosaic covenant and its law played a negative, temporary, and inferior role.

Such teaching immediately leads to further questions. For one, does the Mosaic law continue to play the role of exposing and multiplying sin? Protestantism has generally taught the necessity of leading sinners to conviction by preaching the law before preaching the gospel. The cogency of the fundamental idea here seems obvious. People need to acknowledge that they are sinners before they can be saved, and exposure to God's standards reveals their sin and inability to save themselves. This is in keeping with Paul's argument in Romans 1–3. In fact, there he says that even without the Mosaic law, Gentile people experience conviction from an internal sense of God's moral requirements, what theologians tend to call "natural law" (Rom. 2:14–15).

How does Paul's teaching on the end of the Mosaic law relate to the ongoing use of the law for the purpose of conviction? First, his "negative" statements are looking at "the law" from a historical standpoint—as defining an era in God's program for humanity. There was a time when the central feature in this program was an arrangement that emphasized God's requirements and man's inability to obey them. That arrangement has been left behind, and the main emphasis now is the grace displayed through the work of Jesus Christ.

However, this emphasis does not remove the need for people to know the divine standards they have violated. The question is simply, which standards are in view? That brings us to our second point. In attempting to help people see their sinfulness today, we cannot use the Mosaic law comprehensively and unqualifiedly, since it was so specifically designed for national Israel during a past period. However, it remains useful because, as we will soon see, it embodies so many divine principles of morality that are universally binding.[18]

Perhaps the more troubling question is how people were saved under the Old Covenant. If the law manifested their sin and inability, and the "age of grace" was still future, what hope did the Israelites possibly have? Given that this question is both complex and tangential to our topic, I cannot provide a full discussion here.[19] But let me suggest four factors that would have or should have encouraged an Israelite to cast himself on the grace of God for justification and eternal life. First, the reality that the Mosaic covenant was founded on grace highlighted that God is the One

---

[18]In 1 Timothy 1:9 Paul says that "the law is not made for a righteous man, but for the lawless and disobedient." Furthermore, this use of the law is "according to the glorious gospel of the blessed God" (v. 11). According to one interpretation, this passage speaks of the ongoing use of the law to convict unbelievers of sin in preparation for the gospel. Interestingly, dispensationalist Homer A. Kent Jr. takes this position (*The Pastoral Epistles: Studies in I and II Timothy and Titus* [Chicago: Moody, 1958], 88–89). Others see here the use of the law to restrict sinful behavior and even to guide believers ethically. Compare George W. Knight III, *The Pastoral Epistles: A Commentary on the Greek Text*, The New International Greek Testament Commentary (Grand Rapids: Eerdmans, 1992), 80–92, with William D. Mounce, *Pastoral Epistles*, vol. 46 of Word Biblical Commentary (Nashville: Thomas Nelson Publishers, 2000), 30–44.

[19]For a helpful introduction to this issue, compare Fred H. Klooster, "The Biblical Method of Salvation: A Case for Continuity" with Allen P. Ross, "The Biblical Method of Salvation: A Case for Discontinuity," in *Continuity and Discontinuity: Perspectives on the Relationship Between the Old and New Testaments; Essays in Honor of S. Lewis Johnson*, ed. John S. Feinberg (Wheaton, IL: Crossway, 1988), 131–60, 161–78.

Who initiates a relationship with man. Second, the covenant's sacrificial system taught that God is the One Who provides propitiation and forgiveness. Third, the very inability to obey God's law taught that help must come from outside man.

Finally, the New Covenant promises embedded in the Old Covenant taught the need for divine regeneration in order to obey. For instance, coming out of the gloom of covenant curses, Deuteronomy 30:6 proclaims that one day "the Lord thy God will circumcise thine heart, and the heart of thy seed, to love the Lord thy God with all thine heart, and with all thy soul, that thou mayest live." Though apparently few in number, some Israelites arrived at the right conclusion. Paul emphasizes the testimony of one well-known Old Testament saint: "Even as David also describeth the blessedness of the man, unto whom God imputeth righteousness without works, saying, Blessed are they whose iniquities are forgiven, and whose sins are covered. Blessed is the man to whom the Lord will not impute sin" (Rom. 4:6–8, quoting Ps. 32:1–2).

NOT UNDER THE LAW AS A GENERAL EMPHASIS

Our discussion above leads to one more element in the discontinuity between the Old Covenant and New Covenant eras. We are not under the law as the general emphasis in our relationship with God *after* salvation. One major factor here is the heightened ministry of the Holy Spirit in the New Covenant.[20] Since the New Covenant involves the writing of God's law on our hearts through the Spirit (Jer. 31:33; Ezek. 36:26–27; Heb. 8:10; see below), there is less need for a detailed code to govern conduct. As we have seen, the code itself tends to arouse the flesh instead of restrain it. We need an internal power to subdue our sinful desires, and we have such a power in the person of the indwelling Spirit.

---

[20]For details see Larry D. Pettegrew, *The New Covenant Ministry of the Holy Spirit*, 2nd ed. (Grand Rapids: Kregel, 2001).

This is the thrust of Galatians 5:16–18. After dating the law to a past age, Paul has to come back and explain that we must still be holy. He then tells us how: "This I say then, Walk in the Spirit, and ye shall not fulfil the lust of the flesh. For the flesh lusteth against the Spirit, and the Spirit against the flesh: and these are contrary the one to the other: so that ye cannot do the things that ye would. But if ye be led of the Spirit, ye are not under the law." Notice how "the lust of the flesh" and "the law" are coordinated in contrast with living by means of the Spirit. Trying to be sanctified by law-keeping leads to failure and frustration. Only the Holy Spirit can produce genuine godliness.

In Galatians 6 we find a further perspective on our New Covenant relationship with God. Paul urges, "Bear ye one another's burdens, and so fulfil the law of Christ" (6:2). "The law of Christ" here contrasts with Galatians' many references to the law of Moses. Thus freedom from the Mosaic law does not lead to a lawless life. Rather, it issues in a new kind of law, the law of Christ. The connection with bearing others' burdens and the overall context suggests that love is the central feature of the law of Christ. Paul uses a parallel expression in 1 Corinthians 9:21: "Not being without the law of God but under the law of Christ" (NASB). The New Testament does not provide a comprehensive code labeled "the law of Christ." If anything, we could almost equate this expression with the entire New Testament. The point is that Christ, His redemptive work, and His teaching shape all our ethical decisions.[21] We come to view everything—including the Old Testament law—through the lens of what Jesus did and taught.

---

[21] See further Moo, "Law of Christ," 367–70. Compare David E. Garland, *1 Corinthians*, Baker Exegetical Commentary on the New Testament (Grand Rapids: Baker, 2003), 432.

4

WE ARE UNDER THE LAW

If we keep emphasizing the discontinuity between the Testaments, we will soon be falling off our tightrope. We can begin to steady ourselves by looking again at Galatians 5. That chapter contains some statements that I have purposefully omitted until now. Leading up to the command to walk in the Spirit, Paul says, "For, brethren, ye have been called unto liberty [from the law]; only use not liberty for an occasion to the flesh, but by love serve one another. For all the law is fulfilled in one word, even in this; Thou shalt love thy neighbour as thyself. But if ye bite and devour one another, take heed that ye be not consumed one of another" (Gal. 5:13–15).

Do you notice anything unusual here? Paul views Spirit-produced love as a way of "fulfilling all the law" as summarized in the command of Leviticus 19:18 to love one's neighbor as oneself. That reminds us of what Jesus taught (Matt. 22:36–40): that the two greatest commandments of the law are to love God wholeheartedly (Deut. 6:5) and to love one's neighbor as oneself (Lev. 19:18). Going back to Galatians 5, Paul thinks it is important to point out that "there is no law" against the character qualities produced by the Spirit (v. 23).

Do you see our dilemma? Why should Jesus and Paul be concerned about abiding by the law's standards if in fact the law's jurisdiction has ended? Clearly there must be some significant way in which the actual content of the law remains normative for the New Covenant believer. How can this be? How does this work?

OLD TESTAMENT ANTICIPATION

To answer these questions, we must go back further than we have been in our study—to the very beginning of human history. We must understand why God chose Israel in the first place. Then we need to consider what He promises to do given the nation's failure to fulfill her mission.

The Mission of Israel

The climax of God's creative acts was the creation of man in His image. Since God made man with so many similarities to Himself, He could delegate to him the responsibility of exercising dominion over the earth (Gen. 1:26–28). This reality launches the all-encompassing theme of Scripture—the kingdom of God.[1] Sadly, however, man disobeyed his Maker and plunged his entire race into sin. Genesis 3–11 focuses primarily on the devastating consequences of Adam's choice. But chapter 12 begins to develop how God would fulfill the great "seed" promise of 3:15 to deliver humans from the curse of sin and restore them to a position of fellowship with and usefulness for Him. The Lord's instrument would be a man named Abraham. God repeatedly promised him that he would father a multitude of descendants who would develop into a nation and possess the land of Canaan. However, God did not choose Abraham's people as an end in themselves. Rather, His ultimate purpose was to reach all humanity: "In thee shall all families of the earth be blessed" (12:3).

We know that this promise of universal blessing meant that Jesus Christ, the Savior of the world, would come through Abraham's

---

[1] For a helpful discussion of this theme, see Thurman Wisdom, *A Royal Destiny: The Reign of Man in God's Kingdom* (Greenville, SC: Bob Jones University Press, 2006).

line (Gal. 3:16). But we should also connect God's ethical require-ments with the Abrahamic promises. Genesis 18:18–19 speaks of the righteousness of the covenant family as playing a part in ac-complishing God's worldwide mission. In the context of revealing to Abraham His plan for destroying Sodom, the Lord says,

> . . . Seeing that Abraham shall surely become a great and mighty nation, and all the nations of the earth shall be blessed in him? For I know him, that [i.e., I have chosen him so that] he will command his children and his house-hold after him, and they shall keep the way of the Lord, to do justice and judgment; that the Lord may bring upon Abraham that which he hath spoken of him.

As Christopher J. H. Wright concludes from this passage, God's purpose was "to create a new community of people who in their social life would embody those qualities of righteousness, peace, justice and love that reflect God's character and were God's origi-nal purpose for humanity."[2]

This matter receives more attention four centuries later, when Abraham's descendants are formed into a nation at Mount Sinai. Remember that before laying down the terms of the Mosaic cov-enant, the Lord said, "Now therefore, if ye will obey my voice indeed, and keep my covenant, then ye shall be a peculiar trea-sure unto me above all people: for all the earth is mine: and ye shall be unto me a kingdom of priests, and an holy nation" (Exod. 19:5–6*a*). Note the final phrase "a kingdom of priests, and an holy nation." By definition a priest is a mediator, one who stands be-tween two alienated parties in order to bring them together. That the alienated parties in this passage are God and the non-Israelite

---

[2] *Old Testament Ethics for the People of God* (Downers Grove, IL: InterVarsity, 2004), 51. My entire discussion here is indebted to Wright's analysis.

nations is suggested by the backdrop of Genesis. But the reason "for all the earth is mine" (v. 5) brings this idea to the surface, seemingly indicating that God's choice of Israel is motivated by His concern for the rest of the world.[3]

Again we may begin to think in Christological terms, with Israel serving as the vehicle through which the ultimate Priest would come to accomplish His sacrificial work. But again the primary concern in this context is ethical. The Israelites themselves were to mediate between God and the other nations, and Israel's role is connected with being a holy nation before the others. The laws set forth in chapters 20–23 constitute the initial explanation of what national holiness was to look like. Andreas J. Köstenberger and Peter T. O'Brien elaborate:

> Together the two expressions ["a kingdom of priests, and an holy nation"] indicate that Israel must serve the world by being separate, as a priest served his society by being distinct from it. . . . Israel's calling in Exodus 19:5 had the whole world in view. The nation was to be holy and to serve the world by being separate. Her life was to give clear evidence of Yahweh's rule over her, and thus to be a model of his lordship over the whole world.[4]

Deuteronomy 4:5–8 develops this concept further. As Moses is concluding his ministry, he exhorts the people:

> Behold, I have taught you statutes and judgments, even as the Lord my God commanded me, that ye should do so in the land whither ye go to possess it. Keep therefore and

---

[3]So William J. Dumbrell, *The Search for Order: Biblical Eschatology in Focus* (Grand Rapids: Baker, 1994), 45; compare Sidney Greidanus, "The Universal Dimension of Law in the Hebrew Scriptures," *Studies in Religion* 14 (1985): 40.

[4]*Salvation to the Ends of the Earth: A Biblical Theology of Mission*, New Studies in Biblical Theology 11, ed. D. A. Carson (Downers Grove, IL: InterVarsity, 2001), 34.

do them; for this is your wisdom and your understanding in the sight of the nations, which shall hear all these statutes, and say, Surely this great nation is a wise and understanding people. For what nation is there so great, who hath God so nigh unto them, as the Lord our God is in all things that we call upon him for? And what nation is there so great, that hath statutes and judgments so righteous as all this law, which I set before you this day?

Moses anticipates that Israel's obedience to the Torah would have an attractive influence upon the onlooking nations. Those nations would be impressed by the presence of Yahweh among them and also by the uprightness of their ethical standards. The implication is that the nations would be aroused to seek Yahweh and follow His laws. Eugene H. Merrill confirms: "Even the pagan nations— by whom wisdom was prized and highly sought after—would see in Israel's covenant provisions a wisdom of a higher order, one to be eagerly emulated. This, of course, was part of the attraction of Israel by which they were to become a means of blessing the whole earth (cf. 1 Kings 10:4, 7, 23–24)."[5]

This does not indicate, as theonomists argue, that the particulars of Israel's law were generally intended for every nation in every time, for no other nation enjoyed the same covenant relationship with God.[6] But it seems inescapable that in some significant sense Israel was designed to function as a model for other nations. Merrill rightly captures the balance by focusing on the *wisdom* that underlies the laws, a wisdom that is capable of different applications in different circumstances.

---

[5]*Deuteronomy*, vol. 4 of The New American Commentary (Nashville: Broadman & Holman, 1994), 116–17.

[6]See Vern S. Poythress, *The Shadow of Christ in the Law of Moses* (Phillipsburg, NJ: Presbyterian & Reformed, 1991), 326–29.

As we explore further how this wisdom was conveyed to the nations, I recall my sophomore year in college. That was the year I began to study New Testament Greek. One of the first building blocks we had to master was the conjugation of the verb *luō* ("to loose, destroy"). It seemed as though our teacher interminably shouted the present active indicative forms: "*luō, lueis, luei, luomen, luete, luousi!*" A later teacher gave us bonus points for reviewing the various forms of *luō* printed on a set of cards. Almost twenty years later I can still recite many of those forms with hardly a thought. Why did the instructors insist on our memorizing the forms perfectly? It was not, unfortunately, because every Greek verb looks exactly like *luō*. Rather, that verb was chosen to teach us basic *patterns*—endings, prefixes, and so forth—that would help us analyze similar verbs. To use the technical term, the Greek teachers were using *luō* as a *paradigm*.

The Old Testament law functioned as a paradigm too. In the words of Wright,

> Given, then, on the one hand, Israel's role in relation to God's purpose for the nations, and given, on the other hand, the law's function in relation to that mission of Israel, we can see that the law was designed (along with many other aspects of Israel's historical experience) to mould and shape Israel in certain clearly defined directions, within their own historical and cultural context. That overall social shape, with its legal and institutional structures, ethical norms and values and theological rationale, thus becomes a model or paradigm *that was intended* to have a relevance and application beyond the geographical, historical and cultural borders of Israel itself. . . .

So there is, within the Old Testament itself, an awareness that the law given in a unique way to Israel as a unique people had wider relevance for the rest of humanity. That is, we assume that if God gave Israel certain specific institutions and laws, they were based on principles that have universal validity.[7]

This is the most defensible and balanced way to understand Deuteronomy 4:5–8. By obeying the Torah, Israel would model what God's wisdom/righteousness looked like in her specific covenant and historical-cultural situation. The nations were to derive from this pattern an understanding of ethical principles that God expected them to apply to their own situation. In this sense *all* the Mosaic laws are "moral" because they are concrete expressions of moral truths. More importantly, these truths are themselves expressions of the mind and character of the God Who authored them. Thus ultimately the Torah was designed to teach Israelites and Gentiles about Yahweh Himself.

The New Covenant

If anything is obvious to the reader of the Old Testament, it is that Israel consistently disobeyed the Torah and failed to present to the nations a testimony of divine righteousness. As the Lord Himself says, "I have spread out my hands all the day unto a rebellious people, which walketh in a way that was not good, after their own thoughts" (Isa. 65:2). What is worse, Israel's rebellion caused Yahweh's name to be profaned among the nations (Ezek. 36:20–23). But given God's faithfulness to His word and His commitment to reach the nations through Israel, He devised a plan to ensure the eventual obedience of His chosen people.

This plan has surfaced in our discussion already—the New Covenant. In Jeremiah's "Book of Comfort" (chs. 30–33), the prophet predicts a widespread regeneration and restoration of the

---

[7] *Old Testament Ethics*, 320–21.

Israelites following a period of devastating exile. Here Yahweh says that He will institute a New Covenant that supersedes the Mosaic covenant in a number of ways (31:31–34):

> Behold, the days come, saith the LORD, that I will make a new covenant with the house of Israel, and with the house of Judah: not according to the covenant that I made with their fathers in the day that I took them by the hand to bring them out of the land of Egypt; which my covenant they brake, although I was an husband unto them, saith the Lord: but this shall be the covenant that I will make with the house of Israel; After those days, saith the Lord, I will put my law in their inward parts, and write it in their hearts; and will be their God, and they shall be my people. And they shall teach no more every man his neighbour, and every man his brother, saying, Know the Lord: for they shall all know me, from the least of them unto the greatest of them, saith the Lord: for I will forgive their iniquity, and I will remember their sin no more.

The context also predicts numerous physical blessings connected with Israel's national possession of Palestine. But the spiritual blessings listed in these verses are more fundamental. First, God's law will be internalized. Second, there will be a personal relationship between God and His people. Third, this personal relationship will characterize everyone in the covenant, so that no one will need to urge another to come to know Yahweh. Fourth, this will all be possible because God will effect a final forgiveness of the people's sin.

The first of these blessings is the focal point for our purposes. In contrast to the writing of the Mosaic law on stone tablets at Sinai, the Lord promises, "I will put my law [*torah*] in their inward parts, and write it in their hearts" (v. 33). Ezekiel clarifies that this will happen through a special work of the Holy Spirit: "A new heart also will I give you, and a new spirit will I put within you: and I will take away the stony heart out of your flesh, and I will give you an heart of flesh. And I will put my [S]pirit within you, and cause you to walk in my statutes, and ye shall keep my judgments, and do them" (Ezek. 36:26–27). This internalization of the law is critical to the ultimate fulfillment of Israel's mission. Isaiah's millennial prophecies foresee that one day the nations will travel to Jerusalem to learn Yahweh's *torah* (Isa. 2:2–3; cf. 42:1–4; 51:4–8; Jer. 33:9).

The difficulty is in identifying precisely what Jeremiah means by the *torah* that is placed in people's hearts. We would not want to argue that the New Covenant law is simply a reissuing of the Mosaic law. For one, the New Covenant's absolute forgiveness of sin necessitates a fundamental change in the sacrificial rituals that the Mosaic law established as the means for obtaining forgiveness.[8] Nevertheless, given the Israelite audience of the prophecy, one would expect a strong connection with the Mosaic law. Such a connection seems warranted by the early anticipation of the New Covenant in Deuteronomy 30, which pictures Israel's future return to Yahweh in terms of obedience to Mosaic legislation (vv. 2, 8, 10), principally wholehearted love for God (v. 6).

---

[8]This is a major argument in the most thorough discussion available on the identity of the New Covenant law, Femi Adeyemi, *The New Covenant Torah in Jeremiah and the Law of Christ in Paul*, Studies in Biblical Literature 94 (New York: Peter Lang, 2006), a doctoral dissertation written at Dallas Theological Seminary (cf. "What Is the New Covenant 'Law' in Jeremiah 31:33?" *Bibliotheca Sacra* 163 [2006]: 312–21). Expanding largely on the views of Douglas Moo, Adeyemi argues that Paul's "law of Christ" *is* Jeremiah's New Covenant *torah*. His strong discontinuity case is convincing in many respects, but it does not necessarily rule out the paradigmatic use of the law today (see, for example, *New Covenant Torah*, p. 270, n. 9, and p. 287, n. 279). Adeyemi does not give sufficient attention, however, to this paradigmatic use. For instance, he does not consider the implications of Israel's universalistic role in Deuteronomy 4. In addition, since he limits himself to Paul's "non-contested" books, he does not interact with 2 Timothy 3:14–17.

Here we must recall that the law functioned as a paradigm of wisdom and righteousness that was capable of fresh applications to new situations. With this in mind, the following minimal conclusion seems warranted: *recipients of the New Covenant would receive the internal capacity to live by the transcendent ethical standards upheld in the Mosaic law.* I believe we will find this conclusion substantiated as we turn to the New Testament.

NEW TESTAMENT REALIZATION

The second section of our Bible is more precisely called the New Covenant because everything it teaches relates in some way to the inauguration of the New Covenant promises we have just noted. That the New Covenant is in force today is apparent from several factors. First, at the Last Supper Jesus described His death on the cross with New Covenant terminology (Matt. 26:28; Mark 14:24; Luke 22:20; 1 Cor. 11:25; cf. Heb. 9:20). Second, Paul describes his gospel preaching as the ministry of the New Covenant (2 Cor. 3:6). Third, Hebrews 7–10 strongly urges readers not to return to the Mosaic arrangement because Jesus, the mediator of the New Covenant, has come and performed His work. In fact these chapters quote the prophecy of Jeremiah 31 extensively (Heb. 8:8–12; 10:16–17).

Undoubtedly the originally stated recipients of the New Covenant are ethnic Israelites, and the Lord will fulfill for them everything He said (cf. Rom. 11:25–27). But given that God's purpose has always been to bless all families of the earth through Abraham's descendants (Gen. 12:3), the church presently participates in the spiritual blessings of the New Covenant.[9] This includes the

---

[9]For more on this topic, see the fine study by Rodney J. Decker, "The Church's Relationship to the New Covenant," *Bibliotheca Sacra* 152 (1995): 290–305, 431–56. Decker summarizes his conclusions in "New Covenant, Theology of the," and "New Covenant, Dispensational Views of," *Dictionary of Premillennial Theology*, ed. Mal Couch (Grand Rapids: Kregel, 1996), 278–83.

internalization of God's law, suggesting that the Mosaic law remains relevant as a paradigm in our sanctification. The New Testament emphasizes this relevance by both explicit statements and suggestive examples.

Explicit Statements

In the Sermon on the Mount, Jesus Himself taught both the ongoing relevance of the Torah and a fresh interpretation of it flowing from His arrival. In Matthew 5:17–18 our Lord says, "Think not that I am come to destroy [abolish] the law, or the prophets: I am not come to destroy, but to fulfil. For verily I say unto you, Till heaven and earth pass, one jot or one tittle shall in no wise pass from the law, till all be fulfilled." Commentators have proposed various ways to understand the Greek verb translated "fulfil" in these verses (*plēroō*).[10] But the most solid interpretation is based on the way in which this word is typically used throughout Matthew—to express how Jesus brings into realization Old Testament predictions (e.g., 1:22–23) and patterns (e.g., 2:15). Thus Jesus is claiming that He brings the law and the prophets to their intended consummation. With reference to the law specifically, this means that His teaching unfolds the law's goal or intention and that the law must be interpreted in light of His redemptive work.

The rest of Matthew 5—actually the entire Sermon on the Mount—illustrates how this interpretation should proceed. In particular, Jesus focuses on the internal thrust underlying the law's demands, a thrust that the Pharisees missed by overemphasizing the letter of the law: not hating vs. simply not murdering (vv. 21–26); not lusting vs. simply not committing adultery (vv. 27–30); responding graciously to unfair treatment vs. insisting on our rights (vv. 38–42);

---

[10]For a survey of views and a detailed defense of the position taken here, see D. A. Carson, "Matthew," in *The Expositor's Bible Commentary*, ed. Frank E. Gaebelein (Grand Rapids: Zondervan, 1984), 8:140–45. Compare Poythress, 251–86.

loving our enemies vs. loving only those who love us (vv. 43–48). But our Lord also clarifies ideals to which the law pointed but did not entirely achieve because of its allowance for sinful human nature: the permanence of marriage (vv. 31–32) and absolute honesty (vv. 33–37).

As we adopt this more complete understanding of the righteousness to which the law directed people, Jesus' words in verse 19 become programmatic for the ongoing Christian use of the law: "Whosoever therefore shall break one of these least commandments, and shall teach men so, he shall be called the least in the kingdom of heaven: but whosoever shall do and teach them, the same shall be called great in the kingdom of heaven." Craig L. Blomberg summarizes well Jesus' claim:

> Fulfillment of Scripture, as throughout [Matthew] chaps. 1–4, refers to the bringing to fruition of its complete meaning. Here Jesus views his role as that of fulfilling all of the Old Testament. This claim has massive hermeneutical implications and challenges both classic Reformed and Dispensational perspectives. It is inadequate to say either that none of the Old Testament applies unless it is explicitly affirmed in the New or that all of the Old Testament applies unless it is explicitly revoked in the New. Rather, all of the Old Testament remains normative and relevant for Jesus' followers (2 Tim. 3:16), but none of it can rightly be interpreted until one understands how it has been fulfilled in Christ. Every Old Testament text must be viewed in light of Jesus' person and ministry and the changes introduced by the new covenant he inaugurated.[11]

---

[11] *Matthew*, vol. 22 of The New American Commentary (Nashville: Broadman, 1992), 103–4.

This is basically the same point we saw earlier in Paul's phrase *the law of Christ* (Gal. 6:2; 1 Cor. 9:21). In fact, Thomas R. Schreiner argues that the law of Christ "includes the moral norms of the OT Law."[12]

But we need to look at two more Pauline statements. First are the opening verses of Romans 8. Here the apostle exults in the truth that the work of Christ has delivered us from the authority of the Mosaic law and therefore from bondage to sin and death (vv. 1–3). But then in verse 4 he asserts this surprising purpose for our deliverance: "[in order] that the righteousness of the law might be fulfilled in us, who walk not after the flesh, but after the Spirit." Note the phrase *in us* and the explanatory comment on walking or living according to the Spirit. These factors indicate that Paul is no longer speaking of the imputation of Christ's righteousness to our legal "account" before God. Rather he is describing our practice of the righteousness displayed in the law. Here is a tightrope indeed: Christ delivers us from the defeat, guilt, and condemnation brought by the law so that the Holy Spirit can enable us to live in a way that is in keeping with the ethics revealed in the law.[13]

Paul is even more emphatic in 2 Timothy 3. Verses 16–17 contain His classic teaching on the divine origin, authority, and sufficiency of Scripture: "All scripture is given by inspiration of God, and is profitable for doctrine, for reproof, for correction, for instruction in righteousness: that the man of God may be perfect, throughly

---

[12]"Law of Christ," in *Dictionary of Paul and His Letters*, ed. Gerald F. Hawthorne and Ralph P. Martin (Downers Grove, IL: InterVarsity, 1993), 542.

[13]So Leon Morris, *The Epistle to the Romans*, The Pillar New Testament Commentary (Grand Rapids: Eerdmans, 1988), 303–4; Thomas R. Schreiner, *Romans*, Baker Exegetical Commentary on the New Testament (Grand Rapids: Baker, 1998), 404–8; and to an extent, Douglas J. Moo, *The Epistle to the Romans*, The New International Commentary on the New Testament (Grand Rapids: Eerdmans, 1996), 481–85.

furnished unto all good works." What we might miss, however, is the exact referent of the word *scripture*. In the immediately preceding verses (14–15), Paul has been talking about the holy writings that Timothy grew up learning as a half-Jewish boy—obviously the Old Testament and particularly the Torah. The apostle still has this specific "Scripture" in mind when he goes on to verse 16. Furthermore, the Old Testament seems to remain in view as chapter 4 opens with the command to "preach the word" (v. 2).

It is no wonder, then, that Walter C. Kaiser Jr. calls 2 Timothy 3:16–17 "the most definitive statement from the NT on how the OT is to be used and what roles it must play in the life of believers."[14] Here Paul asserts not only that the Old Testament came from God but also that it remains profitable for teaching doctrine, for identifying and correcting error, and for training in God's righteous standards—all with the goal of producing spiritual maturity and effectiveness in ministry. We would certainly say the same thing of the New Testament Scriptures. In fact, Paul may have intended the word *all* in "all Scripture" to include the New Testament.[15] But even that possibility does not diminish this passage's endorsement of the ongoing use of the Torah in our sanctification.

Suggestive Examples

We have just looked at some passages that encourage us to apply the Old Testament law to our situation as New Testament Christians. But we would greatly benefit from more specific instructions on *how* to do so. The New Testament contains several passages that suggest such instructions by way of example.

---

[14] *Toward Rediscovering the Old Testament* (Grand Rapids: Zondervan, 1987), 26.

[15] George W. Knight III, *The Pastoral Epistles: A Commentary on the Greek Text*, The New International Greek Testament Commentary (Grand Rapids: Eerdmans, 1992), 447–48.

The apostle Peter offers a starting point: a focus on what the law reveals regarding God's character. In summarizing the practical exhortations in the first chapter of his first epistle, Peter writes, "But as he which hath called you is holy, so be ye holy in all manner of conversation; because it is written, Be ye holy; for I am holy" (vv. 15–16). Here he quotes a refrain repeated throughout the book of Leviticus as a motivation for the Israelites to obey Yahweh's laws (11:44–45; 19:2; 20:7, 26). They were to practice separation from sin (actual or symbolic) because their God separated from sin. Stated more broadly, obedience to the law was essentially an imitation of the character of God.

Peter would be the first to discard temporary specifics of Old Testament legislation since he was the one who saw the sheet vision associated with the annulling of Leviticus's food laws (Acts 10:9–16). Yet the Apostle upheld the law as a tool that still reveals God's purity, thus pointing His people to separation from carnal passions (1 Pet. 1:14). Likewise, as we look at any particular Old Testament law, we should ask what it reveals about God—His character, His values, His way of thinking, His heart. This is how the Mosaic Law continues to be paradigmatic. In various ways it reflects timeless truths about God that should guide our behavior.

Truth about God sits right on the surface of many laws, and thus many laws are applicable to the Christian with little or no qualification. Already in the Mosaic period many of the laws in the Torah were absolutes that were binding on other nations. As indicated earlier, the motivation for obeying the sexual prohibitions in Leviticus 18 is avoiding the excruciating punishment the Canaanites were facing for violating these same laws (vv. 24–29). In other words, God was holding Israelites and non-Israelites to the same standards of sexuality. Likewise, in the oracles that Israel's proph-

WE ARE UNDER THE LAW

ets issued against Gentile nations, the accusations overlap with Mosaic legislation (Isa. 13–23; Jer. 46–51; Ezek. 25–32; Amos 1–2). In fact, Amos pronounces judgment on Israel for the same type of cruelty that brings condemnation on Syria, Philistia, Tyre, Edom, Ammon, and Moab. Since we have no reason to think that the Lord has changed His mind about laws of this type, we can say that they apply directly to the Christian.

The New Testament contains various examples of such laws, some of which we have noted already. Jesus taught that we must still obey the injunction of Deuteronomy 6:5 to love God wholeheartedly (Matt. 22:35–38). He also affirmed that we must obey Leviticus 19:18 and love our neighbor as we love ourselves (Matt. 22:39). Paul emphasized this second obligation and pointed out that such love for neighbor will result in our keeping the last five of the Ten Commandments (Rom. 13:8–10). Such love would actually fulfill the essence of "every other commandment" (v. 9) or "all the law" (Gal. 5:14).

Ephesians 6 provides another striking example. Here Paul urges Christian children to obey the fifth commandment of the Decalogue: "Honour thy father and mother; (which is the first commandment with promise;) that it may be well with thee, and thou mayest live long on the earth" (Eph. 6:2–3). But notice how the apostle has changed Exodus 20:12's "the land which the Lord thy God giveth thee" (Canaan) to "the earth." This minor adaptation was necessary because the Ephesians lived in Asia Minor and were not heirs to the land of Palestine. Yet in spite of the discontinuities, Paul urges the same standard on Gentile children and sees the same basic consequences at work today. A less familiar example relates to the Torah's jurisprudence regulations. The law required two or three witnesses to establish an accusation in court (Num. 35:30; Deut. 17:6; 19:15). Both Jesus (Matt. 18:16) and Paul (1 Tim. 5:19) brought this law over into the procedures for church discipline.

Many Old Testament laws are not so easy to handle, however. What should we do with laws that are so specific to Israel's situation that they cannot be followed directly? Here again we find help in the New Testament. In 1 Corinthians 9 Paul is defending the right of gospel preachers to accept financial remuneration for their ministry. Naturally he uses the Old Testament argument that the priests and Levites ate from the animals that were offered as sacrifices (v. 13). But his primary argument (vv. 8–11) is not this straightforward:

> Say I these things as a man? or saith not the law the same also? For it is written in the law of Moses, Thou shalt not muzzle the mouth of the ox that treadeth out the corn. Doth God take care for oxen? Or saith he it altogether [surely] for our sakes? For our sakes, no doubt, this is written: that he that ploweth should plow in hope; and that he that thresheth in hope should be partaker of his hope. If we have sown unto you spiritual things, is it a great thing if we shall reap your carnal [material] things?

This passage quotes Deuteronomy 25:4, which required farmers to allow oxen to eat from the grain they were threshing. Paul denies that God's concern here was merely or even primarily the oxen. Rather His ultimate goal was to promote a spirit of generous concern for the needs of others, as was evident throughout the laws of Deuteronomy 25. If the Lord expected such a spirit to be shown toward animals, how much more would He desire that Christians provide for the physical needs of those who are working to meet their spiritual needs? Thus the law was written "for our sakes" in the sense that it illustrates a universal principle that applies to a different but parallel circumstance.[16]

Following Paul's lead in 1 Corinthians 9, a number of scholars have suggested helpful methodologies for sifting through the covenantal, religious, cultural, political, and geographical differences between Israel and the church, in order to discern the underlying truths and make legitimate applications. For example, Wright offers the following steps that are illustrated at length in his work.

First, *"distinguish the different kinds of law in the text."*[17] This is not a reintroduction of the moral-civil-ceremonial framework, since every law is ultimately moral. Rather, it is an attempt to identify natural classifications that will help us to study the law in its original social context. Wright himself suggests five categories: criminal law; case law ("if . . . then" legislation); family law; cultic (religious) law, further subdivided into sacrificial, sacred calendar, and symbolic (e.g., food) laws; and compassionate law (e.g., care of widows and orphans).[18]

Second, *"analyse the social function and relative status of particular laws and institutions. . . .* Such enquiry prevents us from treating every text with flat equality and enables us to discern those laws or values that were treated with greater priority in Israel itself. This ought to give us some guidance in our own scale of relative moral values."[19]

---

[16]See further David E. Garland, *1 Corinthians*, Baker Exegetical Commentary on the New Testament (Grand Rapids: Baker, 2003), 409–11; compare Walter C. Kaiser Jr., *The Uses of the Old Testament in the New* (Chicago: Moody, 1985), 203–20.

[17]*Old Testament Ethics*, 321.

[18]Ibid., 288–301.

[19]Ibid., 322.

Third, *"define the objective(s) of the law in Israelite society."* Wright recommends the following specific questions to arrive at the objective(s):

- What kind of situation was this law trying to promote, or prevent?

- Whose interests was this law aiming to protect?

- Who would have benefited from this law and why?

- Whose power was this law trying to restrict, and how did it do so?

- What rights and responsibilities were embodied in this law?

- What kind of behaviour did this law encourage or discourage?

- What vision of society motivated this law?

- What moral principles, values or priorities did this law embody or instantiate?

- What motivation did this law appeal to?

- What sanction or penalty (if any) was attached to this law, and what does that show regarding its relative seriousness or moral priority?[20]

Fourth, *"preserve the objective but change the context."* In other words, determine contemporary applications to "comparable situations, interests, needs, powers, rights, behaviours, and so on." Applications to individual and church decisions will be easier to discern than a Christian posture toward issues in society at large. Not everyone will be comfortable with Wright's social emphasis, but his main point deserves to be heard in a church increasingly influenced by a relativistic culture: "The more sharply we can ar-

---

[20]Ibid., 322–23.

ticulate the very particularity of Israel and understand the reasons for the laws they had, the more confident we can be in making 'authorized' ethical choices; that is, choices that are legitimate within the contours and limits of the paradigm God has given us."[21]

---

[21] Ibid., 323–24. For further suggestions on methodology and specific examples, see the works by Dorsey, Kaiser, and Sprinkle referenced in notes 44–46 of chapter 2 above. Within the Dutch Reformed tradition, Albert M. Wolters has also made some insightful comments regarding the contemporary use of the law. He writes, for instance, "God did the implementing for his people in the Old Testament, while in the New he in large measure gives us the freedom in Christ to do our own implementing. That is the point of Paul's letter to the Galatians. But in both cases he holds us to the blueprint of the law of creation. In the Old Testament the explanations he gave included detailed instructions for the implementation of the blueprint; that was by way of apprenticeship. In Christ we are journeyman builders—still bound to the architect's explicit directions, but with considerable freedom of implementation as new situations arise." *Creation Regained: Biblical Basics for a Reformational Worldview* (Grand Rapids: Eerdmans, 1985), 35. Also worth consulting is Graeme Goldsworthy, *Preaching the Whole Bible as Christian Scripture* (Grand Rapids: Eerdmans, 2000), 152-66. Building on his various works on the kingdom of God and redemptive history, Goldsworthy makes some helpful suggestions regarding the Christological dimensions of the Mosaic law. In the process he stresses the discontinuity between the Testaments, criticizing the Protestant catechisms for their direct importing of the Ten Commandments into the Christian life. "However," he writes, "there is no doubt that the case can be made that the New Testament assumes continuity of the ethical law of Israel and nowhere repudiates it but rather sharpens the application of it" (154). Later he encourages a cautious use of the Reformers' three uses of the law (166).

5.

CONCLUSION

Our study has brought us to the following understanding of the tightrope of law and grace. On the one hand, the law does not have direct covenantal authority over us. Christ's work ended the Mosaic covenant and the time period dedicated particularly to exposing human sinfulness. On the other hand, instructed by Jesus and enabled by the Spirit, we must continue to use the law paradigmatically as we seek to imitate and please God in the New Covenant age—because all the laws in the Torah are based on timeless truths regarding God's character and will. Or, as David A. Dorsey puts it, all the laws remain binding "in a revelatory and pedagogical sense."[1]

This summary brings us to some practical observations regarding the ongoing use of the law. For one, we must guard against so emphasizing the law that we lose the blessing of living under the New Covenant. As we saw in Galatians 5, the law itself does not sanctify; the Holy Spirit does. Obedience to the law's principles is the outflow of faith in Christ and yieldedness to the Spirit. It is not the essence of our relationship to God. In fact it was apparently to preserve us from a performance mindset that Paul spoke of our "fulfilling" the intent of the law instead of actually "doing" the law (Rom. 8:4; 13:8–10; Gal. 5:14).[2]

---

[1] "The Use of the OT Law in the Christian Life: A Theocentric Approach," *Evangelical Journal* 17 (1999), 4.

[2] See Douglas J. Moo, "The Law of Christ as the Fulfillment of the Law of Moses: A Modified Lutheran View," in *Five Views on Law and Gospel*, ed. Wayne G. Strickland

Nevertheless, relating to God does include the use of His self-revelation in the law. And we do not need the New Testament to comment on an Old Testament law in order to find it applicable. Instead we should follow the pattern the New Testament sets forth in handling the selected laws discussed in chapter 4 above. This process entails hard work, and sometimes our conclusions must remain tentative. But consider three factors that should motivate the diligence required.

First, careful attention to the Torah's laws displays devotion to the God Who wrote them and Whom they reveal. Second, though the law's specificity can be challenging, it shows us that God is concerned about the details of His people's lives.[3] Third, if our applications are correct, they carry the force of divine authority. As John M. Frame writes, "Once we discover a true application of Scripture, that application is unconditionally binding. No one has the right to say, for example, 'I won't steal, but I will embezzle, since the prohibition of embezzling is only an "application".' "[4] Likewise Paul would not tolerate the Corinthians' responding that his use of Deuteronomy 25:4 was merely his personal application of the text (1 Cor. 9:8–11).

To appreciate further the weight of rightly deduced applications, we need to consider again the original recipients of the law. Contrary to the impression we often get from reading the Pentateuch, the Mosaic law does not legislate every possible circumstance the Israelites might face. God was expecting that even they would think paradigmatically and make applications to new situations.

(Grand Rapids: Zondervan, 1999), 359–60; idem, "The Law of Moses or the Law of Christ," in *Continuity and Discontinuity*, 208–10.

[3]See further John Goldingay, *Approaches to Old Testament Interpretation*, rev. ed. (Downers Grove, IL: InterVarsity, 1990), 51–55.

[4]*The Doctrine of the Knowledge of God* (Phillipsburg, NJ: Presbyterian & Reformed, 1987), 68.

Douglas K. Stuart has suggested some examples that make this point humorously:

> No Israelite could say, "The law says I must make restitution for stolen oxen or sheep (Exod. 22:1) but I stole your goat; I don't have to pay you back," or "The law says that anyone who attacks his father or mother must be put to death (Exod. 21:15) but I attacked my grandmother, so I shouldn't be punished," or "The law says that certain penalties apply for hitting someone with a fist or a stone (Exod. 21:18), but I kicked my neighbor with my foot and hit him with a piece of wood, so I shouldn't be punished." Such arguments would have insulted the intelligence of all concerned and made no impact on those rendering judgments.[5]

Building on these illustrations, we can challenge contemporary views of "legalism." To elevate the law (Old Testament or otherwise) to a primary or central role in our relationship with God tends to legalism indeed. Often, however, accusations of legalism come simply for practicing or insisting on standards that are not specifically spelled out in Scripture. But one must ask, who is actually better oriented to law—the one who strives to understand the spirit and principles of God's laws and then applies those to the specifics of modern life, or the one who demands a black-and-white verse before he feels compelled to obey? Which one is more concerned about understanding and pleasing the Lawgiver—as opposed to fulfilling the bare letter of the law? Surely, working out the many implications of the law's moral truths is part of what the psalmist has in mind in his idyllic description of the godly man (Ps. 1:2):

> But his delight is in the Torah of the Lord;
> And in his Torah doth he meditate day and night.

---

[5]"Preaching from the Law," in *Preaching the Old Testament*, ed. Scott M. Gibson (Grand Rapids: Baker, 2006), 95–96.